YEHUDI MENUHIN M

The Bassoon

William Waterhouse

KAHN & AVERILL, LONDON

First published in 2003 by
Kahn & Averill
9 Harrington Road, London SW7 3ES

Reprinted 2005, 2011

British Library Cataloguing in Publication Data

A catalogue record for this book is available from the British Library

ISBN 1-871082-68-4

9 781871 082685

Typeset in Times by YHT Ltd., London
Printed in Great Britain by
Halstan & Co Ltd., Amersham, Bucks

Contents

Contents

Preface

This book, which represents a somewhat personal view of bassoon-playing, is one that the late Lord Menuhin had originally commissioned for his series of 'Guides' thirty years ago in October 1973. Although I made considerable progress with it at that time I found myself unable to finish it for various reasons, and allowed the project to lapse. In 1995 my publisher Morris Kahn, having recently acquired the rights to the series, started to commission supplementary volumes and offered me a second chance to complete this task. That it has finally appeared is entirely due to his initiative, persistence and patient forbearance.

At this somewhat later stage of my career I feel more confident about sharing with others my experiences as player and teacher. The book is designed for the more advanced student rather than the beginner. In his original letter Yehudi Menuhin had expressed a wish that "the reader may gain at least an understanding of its (the bassoon's) use, enough to become a better listener and at best to encourage the sympathetic reader to study the instrument itself". I hope that it will not be found wanting either in that respect.

Acknowledgments are due to my professional colleagues – many of whom are listed in Appendix I – former students and friends. These include Richard Moore (Waterlooville), who has painstakingly scrutinized the entire text and made a number of valuable contributions to it, Prof. Dr Giles Brindley FRS (London), Matthew Dart (London), Dr

Preface

Charles Lipp (Chicago IL) and Hugh Rosenbaum (London); Elizabeth Scott-Taggart supplied much of the art work. Most of all I wish to thank my Three Ladies:- Ms Kari Krueger-Shea (Annapolis MD) and Frau Ann-Katrin Zimmermann (Tübingen) for all the practical assistance and advice they generously gave over the course of many months – and my wife Elisabeth.

William Waterhouse
February 2003

Introduction

"What on earth ever made you take up the instrument?" is a question every bassoonist is liable to be asked. The reasons may be many and varied. Some will have been attracted right from the start by its tone-colour and musical personality. Others will have become bassoonists for no better reason than that they were drafted onto it at school when an instrument became available; such a shot-gun introduction might not always lead to a lasting relationship. A somewhat more auspicious background is where the player has had the opportunity to try his hand first at other instruments – in my own case I graduated to it downwards, via the clarinet and bass-clarinet. Luckily there is usually time for such trial engagement periods, as it is not vital (as it is in the case of stringed instruments) to specialise before one's teens.

The bassoon has much to offer that can satisfy the prospective player; while in the string quartet the best vantage point from which to gain an insider's view of what is going on is from the viola player's chair – which is why it was this instrument that Haydn and Mozart preferred to play – in the orchestra the bassoon occupies a comparable position. Then there is the tone itself, which has been traditionally considered to bear the closest resemblance of any musical instrument to the human voice, and well able to express a wide range of feeling – from plaintive melancholy on the one hand to wit and humour on the other. There is also the role which the bassoon is called upon to play in the

Introduction

orchestra; thanks to its extensive range, it fulfils the role of both tenor and bass to the woodwind choir – and occasionally also that of alto. While its share of solo material is less than that of its higher-pitched brethren, there is in most orchestral works sufficient matter to hold ones attention, while at the same time allowing the opportunity to take an intelligent interest in what is going on around. Composers such as Haydn, Mozart and Beethoven demonstrated a particular understanding and affection for the instrument in their orchestral writing; their works are especially enjoyable and rewarding for the bassoonist to play.

Where solo repertoire is concerned, we can hardly deny that the bassoon is less well off than most of the other winds. We do not possess sonatas by Bach, Beethoven or Brahms, though there is a wide range of offerings by lesser composers. Where concertos with orchestra are concerned we have, it is true, examples by Vivaldi, Mozart and Weber – but little else of comparable calibre. The prospect is brighter when we turn to chamber music. Not only does our instrument appear generally in works for winds – from wind trios and quintets to sextets and octets for wind band – but it also features in such masterpieces for mixed combinations as Schubert's Octet and Beethoven's Septet. There is also a modest repertoire for bassoon and string trio as well as pieces for bassoons only – which at least are rewarding for the player. The bassoonist can usually be sure of a welcome in amateur music-making circles on account of his scarcity value. Not for him the problem encountered by flautists and clarinettists in finding opportunities to play in amateur orchestras. It used to be said that possession of an instrument guaranteed employment, while knowing how to play it was an added bonus ... !

To sum up: while the bassoon hardly counts as a *prima donna* among instruments, it does nonetheless offer considerable rewards to the discriminating player.

If these then are the rewards, what are the problems and challenges that confront the prospective player? First of all he or she has to be equipped with an instrument and face the problem of obtaining something suitable. Bassoons cost more to make than almost any other wind instrument; the fact that they command a comparatively small market contributes to this cost. They can be idiosyncratic, which tends to make players faithful to a particular instrument once it has been 'worked in', making for a slow turn-over of good second-hand instruments. Until recently there was arguably no such thing as an instrument that did not possess at least one or two troublesome notes (in this respect cheap instruments were even worse than expensive ones); the response of certain notes could be treacherous, even for the expert. However the last decades have seen great advances in the study and understanding of bassoon acoustics on the part of makers. Most new instruments show a marked improvement in such matters as intonation and evenness together with an increase in available tone-colour and dynamic.

By its nature, the bassoon is demanding on those who wish to play it. There is its size and weight to consider. The relative distance from each other of the holes and keys, while somewhat less than on archaic models, nevertheless requires a certain size of hand and stretch of finger. The modern instrument is designed for an adult of average dimensions; problems can arise if the player is too small or too big for that matter; 'custom' modifications can help in many cases – particularly the so-called 'short-reach' models. As regards weight, the problems inherent in the use of the traditional neck-strap can be alleviated by using other means of support – chest harness, spike, seat-strap, leg-rest etc. The depth and range of its compass is demanding on the player's breath capacity making it unsuitable for starting at too tender an age. In the 19th century, a smaller version of the instrument was sometimes used for young beginners. Since the 1990s a higher-pitched child's model has been developed that allows them to start as young as eight years of age; however the early teens is probably young enough to start learning. If the beginner has already had experience on another instrument, this can be a decided advantage; instruments such as the clarinet will have trained the lips in strength, and the piano the fingers in independence. The recorder, particularly the alto and bass, can also afford advantages for the prospective bassoonist; devoid of reed problems, by being based in the key of F they share much in common with bassoon fingering.

Due to its unusual acoustics, fingering is more complex than on other woodwinds; all ten fingers are involved in what are often inconsistent patterns of use. Fingers have often several different key-touches to control: the left thumb, for example, has as many as nine keys to cope with both alone and in different combinations. Finger technique will probably be the hardest aspect of the instrument facing the mature beginner. Then there are the varied and varying problems presented by the reed, on which so much appears to depend. Tone is another important factor; it must be admitted that the range of dynamic achievable on the bassoon is modest compared with most other wind instruments. The player must often cope with subtle problems of balance – being told one moment that he is inaudible, and a moment later that he is too loud.

Is the bassoon then especially difficult to play? I remember many years ago having teased a senior colleague who held strong views on this subject by attempting to deny that this was so. He replied vehemently: "You must never say that!", and proceeded to tell me how at Kneller Hall, the conservatoire of the British Army where he taught bassoon, trainee bandmasters had to pass a proficiency test on every instrument, being allotted one month's tuition on each to do so. He had however succeeded in persuading the authorities that, because of the superior difficulties of our instrument, a double allocation of two months was necessary for his students!

Notwithstanding his reproach, I would maintain that the bassoon need present no special difficulties that cannot be successfully dealt with once they have been properly comprehended. This book attempts to analyse and elucidate the basic principles of playing. Occasionally a somewhat doctrinaire approach has been adopted, which attempts to distinguish between 'right' and 'wrong', between 'good' and 'bad'; in these cases the reader is invited to draw an analogy between playing and other comparable 'sporty' disciplines. The principles expressed reflect my own personal convictions, which inevitably derive from my experiences as student, performer and teacher (which are elaborated in Appendix §7.1).

I hope that the book will serve both as guide and stimulus, not only for the comparative beginner but more especially for the advanced student as well. May it encourage the study of an instrument that will always be found rewarding to those who respond to its essential nature and to the role it is called upon to play in music.

Key to Notation of Pitch

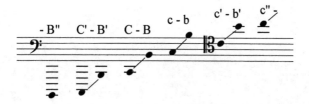

One
History

Introduction

This chapter provides an overview of the history of the bassoon. An awareness of this is valuable, particularly when we interpret music from earlier periods or become involved in playing period instruments. For a more detailed account of the history of our instrument the reader is referred to such works as Langwill's *The Bassoon and Contrabassoon* (Langwill, 1965), the author's relevant article in *The New Grove Dictionary of Music & Musicians* (Waterhouse, 2\2001), and other texts cited in §6.1.

In trying to chart bassoon history we need to remember that the evidence available resembles a jigsaw puzzle of which only a few pieces survive. Tempting as it is to try to fit these together, all too often this is a fruitless task that may lead to wrong conclusions. Prime evidence would be in the form of actual specimens; however when we start looking for these, we soon become aware of problems. Always expensive to produce, they were seldom made in comparable quantities to other types in greater demand. Of those that survive, few are in their original state, often showing the signs of generations of use. In consequence, many have suffered alteration in an attempt to keep pace with the constant rise in pitch. Having seldom been supplied with a durable case they have lost such vital accessories as crook and reed. They have suffered damage from wet-rot and woodworm – unlike the boxwood used for

1

other woodwinds, maple falls an easy prey to such damage. For these reasons bassoons survive in comparatively small numbers, while those that do are hardly representative. Paradoxically an instrument considered good in its time would have been kept in service until it wore out, when it would be discarded. There are virtually no survivors at all from before the 18th century. The only other evidence available is in the form of written documents and pictorial sources, and here we are better served. From the earliest times inventories and archival records help to document the use of the instrument and those who played it. Ambiguities of nomenclature pose a problem; in the earliest period we cannot always be sure to which instrument a given name refers. This is where iconographic evidence is invaluable.

The bassoon (Fr. *basson*, Ger. *Fagott*, It. *fagotto*) shares two design features that distinguish it from other woodwinds. Rather than consisting of a straight tube extending no further than just beyond the sixth fingerhole, the bassoon's bore extends way beyond this point for more than half of its total length; it is also folded back upon itself. Two basic forms of construction can be distinguished:

- the earlier dulcian, built essentially in one piece, used from the early 1500s to the early 1700s (with the exception of Spain, see below)
- the jointed bassoon, which came into use in the late 17th century.

The period of overlap is documented by an engraving of 1698 showing a Nuremberg woodwind maker's workshop; the craftsman seated at his bench is surrounded by tools and instruments, amongst which we can recognize a 4-jointed model of bassoon, while the instrument he is working on is a dulcian (Pl 1).

Plate 1
Dulcian and bassoon manufacture: the woodwind-maker, from *Abhandlung der Gemein-Nützlichen Haupt-Stände* by Johann Christoph Weigel, Nuremburg 1698.

Dulcian

Its name probably refers to the fact that its tone was more subdued than that of the other reed instruments of the time (Latin *dulcis*, 'agreeable' or 'soft') . With this instrument the length of the sounding tube is folded back on itself within a single shaft of wood. While the crook was relatively short, the bell was often flared and detachable. The earliest mentions of such an instrument are from early 16th century Italy. In 1516 Cardinal Ippolito I d'Este, known as

3

The Bassoon

a keen patron of innovation in the arts, employed 'Gerardo francese' in Ferrara as a player of the *fagoth*. In 1532 the inventor Afranio demonstrated in nearby Mantua a type of bagpipe that he confusingly called a *phagotus* (the derivation of this name remains unclear), for which reason he was long credited with having invented the bassoon.

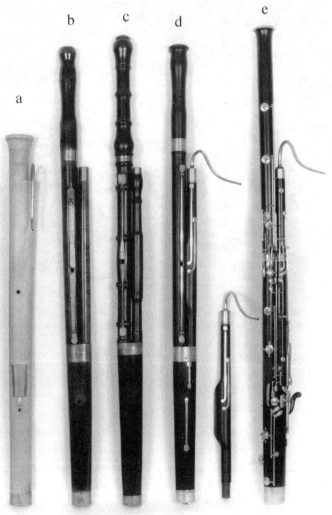

Plate 2

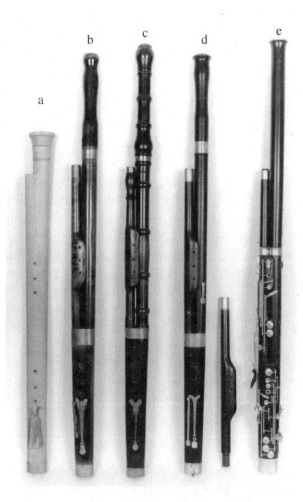

Plate 3
Plates 2 and 3 Historic bassoons (author's collection):
a   2-key *Bass-Dulzian*, copy of original by 'HIERO.S', ?Venice/London late 16th
    century (Augsburg #3014), by Rainer Weber, Bayerbach 1999
b   4-key Baroque Bassoon by Thomas Stanesby (ca1668-1734), London 1st ¼
    18th century; the earliest known English-made bassoon
c   3-key Baroque *Fagott* by Meister HKI.C.W., ?Thuringia early 18th century
d   7-key Classical *Fagott* by Johann Friedrich Floth (1761-1807), Dresden
    1803/06; keys and mounts in silver, complete with *corps de rechange*
    (alternative joint) and matching unperforated crooks
e   *Reformfagott* by Friedrich Wilhelm Kruspe (1838-1911), Erfurt; 3-jointed
    model (1892 patent) with many noteworthy original features.

The Bassoon

Our earliest sighting of the dulcian is on an alabaster relief commissioned for a monument carved in Flanders erected in 1563 in Freiberg Cathedral by the King of Saxony. In early times all woodwinds were built in different sizes. A surviving set of dulcians in Augsburg comprises five different sizes, from descant to octave bass. The most used size, known in Germany as the *Choristfagott*, also survives today in the largest numbers (Pls 2a, 3a). This instrument had eight finger-holes and two open keys whose mechanism was concealed under a protective brass box, with a range from C to f'. The 'swallow-tail' shape of the little finger key allowed the instrument to be held either to the left or right of the body. This compact 8'-register instrument, easily manageable on the march, soon replaced the straight bass shawm to become the standard bass to the woodwind group during the following century. Works by composers such as Bertoli and Böddecker published in the second quarter of the 17th century show the instrument in a virtuoso soloistic role. While in other parts of Western Europe this instrument had dropped out of use by around 1700, it continued to be used in Spain for liturgical purposes until the early 20th century.

Transitional

It is tempting to presume an evolution whereby, throughout Europe, the unwieldy bass shawm was developed into the uncomplicated-looking folded dulcian, which was in turn replaced by the jointed bassoon. This theory fails to explain why the dulcian's smooth simple form should be given the name 'fagotto', which in France appeared to refer to a 'bundle of sticks'. If this derivation were correct, the explanation might be that, in this country, there were indeed alternative intermediate stages of design, prior to the emergence of the bassoon, when makers were addressing how to fold the bore of the shawm in half. By description and illustration Mersenne (1636) indicates how these problems may have been tackled. Essentially a long conical bore was cut into two and the halves laid adjacent, secured together by bands of brass or leather wrapping with the two bores linked by a hole drilled laterally at the base. He then goes on to say that they were "different from the preceeding bass (shawm) only in that they break into two parts to be able to be managed and carried more easily; that is why they are called Fagots because they resemble two pieces of wood which are bound and faggotted together". Evidence is lacking regarding the existence of the dulcian in France, and this type of intermediate-stage instrument might have been this country's route from the bass shawm to the four-jointed bassoon (it being only in France that such a transitional stage between the dulcian and the four-jointed instrument can be identified).

Baroque

As in the case of the dulcian, it is not possible to state categorically when and where the jointed 3/4-keyed instrument originated, the range of which now descended to B♭′. It has traditionally been held that the Baroque woodwinds, including bassoon, were developed in France in the second half of the 17th century by members of the Hotteterre family. In Paris Lully scored for the *basson* (range B♭′ to f′) in his opera *Psyché* of 1678, pioneering the antiphonal use of wind and string groups. By 1731 Rameau was employing it as high as b♮′ as an independent voice. These new French instruments, built to a flat pitch of around 390Hz, were externally plain and lacking in ornament. Although evidently produced in large quantities, not a single example has survived. It was French woodwind players, employed at court and in the theatre, who by the

7

1680s had introduced the new *basson* to England. The earliest surviving native-built instrument (Stanesby *fl.* London 1691-1734) has a French bell profile and German key design (Pls 2b, 3b).

Another impulse appears to have emanated from Amsterdam. An unsigned Dutch painting *Der Fagottspieler* in Aachen (Pl 4), datable to the late 17th century, shows a model identifiable with a 3-keyed instrument by the leading Dutch maker Richard Haka, which is preserved in Sondershausen. In Germany Denner and Schell had been copying French oboe and recorder models in Nuremberg since ca 1684 and Denner's bassoons are the earliest we can attribute to an identifiable workshop. Surviving instruments are remarkable for their decorative turning; some of the rings are purely aesthetic, while others serve as key mountings (Pls 2c, 3c). The end of the bell, with an inverse-taper choke, sometimes conceals a bulbous cavity like that of an english horn. For most instruments maple was used, although ebony, boxwood and fruitwood was used for more expensive models. The crook, longer and thicker than that of today, was unperforated. The reed used was wide, about as long as the middle finger, and built on a staple – like that of the oboe. In preparation most of the cane was removed on the inside, while flat-scraped externally; the resulting horseshoe, without heart, could thus vibrate freely between the rigid edges of bark enframing it under the direct control of the lips. As with the dulcian, the way of holding the instrument was not standardized, the swallow-tail touch of the little finger key permitting its use by either hand. The addition of the 4th key, soon added to improve the forked G♯, determined which side of the body the instrument had to be held – although the swallow-tail persisted.

Plate 4
Early bassoon: *Der Fagottspieler* (Aachen, Suermondt Museum). The model of
instrument resembles that of Haka (Amsterdam) rather than of Denner
(Nuremburg). Attributed to Harmen Hals, and thus dateable to ca1667,
stylistically the painting belongs to a group representing half-length figures of
popular characters (peasant smoking pipe, drinker etc.); here a bassoonist
appears to be taking snuff.

Classical

It was modifications to the bore and wall thickness, rather
than the addition of keys, that changed the function of the
instrument from that of a continuo-type bass into an

expressive tenor voice. The adoption of a 'harmonic key' on the wing joint, first documented in 1787, facilitated the higher register; this was often added to existing instruments. Dresden-made instruments by Grenser and Grundmann, esteemed for their round and pleasing tone, became the most sought after. They were supplied with up to three wing joints of differing length and as many crooks in order to allow for differences of pitch. The standard 7-key model, on which low B♮′ and C♯ were unobtainable, remained in use up until the mid 19th century (Pls 2d, 3d).

Almenräder / Heckel

Gottfried Weber's study of woodwind acoustics, the first of modern times, appeared in 1816. The Mainz bassoonist Carl Almenräder (1786-1843) was the first to implement these theories by commissioning the local factory, Schott, to execute his designs. His main innovations were to the lower half of the bore where from below A the tone-holes were shifted, enlarged and added to. His 15-keyed model of 1817 not only extended the range chromatically from B♭′ to g″ but also improved intonation, evenness and projection. In 1831 in partnership with Johann Adam Heckel (1812-1877) he opened the workshop which, under the latter's grandson Wilhelm Heckel (1879-1952) (Pl 5), first achieved its incomparable reputation worldwide. Differing models were developed during the second half of the 19th century in Vienna, Stuttgart and Coblenz, and more radical Boehm-inspired 'reform' models in London, Paris and Erfurt (Pls 2e, 3e). It is however the *Heckelfagott* and its imitators that has remained dominant.

19th Century France

In France the instrument failed ever to undergo a reform comparable to that of Almenräder and has thus retained

Plate 5
Bassoon-maker Wilhelm Hermann Heckel (1879-1952);
photographed 1937 in Biebrich.

most of the essential features of the late 18th century
basson. The Parisian player Cugnier wrote in 1780 that its
tone required 'bite' (*mordant*) in order to have the necessary timbre and, by comparison with German timbre, this

11

element of reediness remained in favour for many years. The leading maker Savary (*fl.* Paris 1816-1853), whose instruments were also much admired in England, devised an ingenious ratchet-driven slide for tuning. His contemporary Simiot (*fl.* Lyon 1808-1844) in 1817 was the first to replace the butt cork with a metal U-tube. Extra keys were progressively added, mostly to replace the traditional fork-fingering of accidentals. Eugène Jancourt (1815-1892), the outstanding virtuoso, teacher and composer for his instrument, collaborated from 1850 onwards with the leading Paris makers to produce by 1879 an improved 22-key model. It is this model – with re-sited 6th tone-hole and made of palissander-wood – that has remained, with only minor modifications, the standard *basson* to this day. Copied by makers in Belgium, England and Italy, it was in use in these countries until well into the next century.

The 20th Century

This century saw comparatively few innovations carried out to either model. From the late 1930s synthetics were used to replace maple-wood (*Plexiglas* in Germany, polypropylene in the US). Sporadic efforts were made to re-design key-work (Gheorghe Cuciureanu, Venceslav Bubnovich), the tone-hole lattice (Zoltan Lukacs and Edgar Brown), and incorporate electrics (Giles Brindley). Research yielded fresh insights into bassoon acoustics (Arthur Benade, Walter Krüger), manufacture (Don Christlieb, Alan Fox), and reed-cane (Jean-Marie Heinrich). Crook devices fitted included the whisper-key (Wilhelm Heckel) and the 'altissimo key' (Otto Steinkopf *et al.*). The main effort has been to help the bassoon deliver the ever-increasing volume level required by a modern symphony orchestra now dominated by wide-bore brass instruments.

A notable change has been the relative distribution worldwide of *Fagott* and *basson*. Until the 1930s it was only in German-speaking lands, Russia, Manchester in England and a few cities in America that the German instrument was in use professionally. By the 1960s the *Fagott* had replaced the French *basson* throughout the world with the exception of parts of Switzerland and Belgium, Brazil, and in France. Even in this latter country the native model has been forced to yield ground to the German instrument in a number of orchestras and conservatoires – as well as among the ranks of amateurs. There are many reasons for this. Modern trends towards globalization inevitably lead to the loss of national character. The *basson*, in spite of recent efforts to improve power and compatibility by carrying out modifications to instrument, bocal and reed, has failed to compete with a rival that is more user-friendly and reliable, and with a less complicated fingering system.

Two
The Bassoon & Relations

§2.1 The modern German *Fagott*

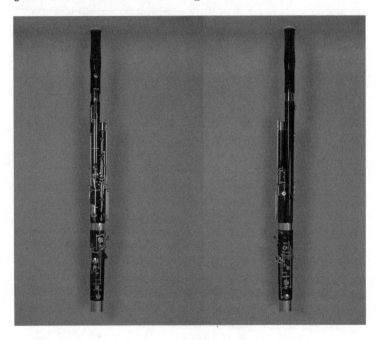

Plate 6
Modern *Fagott* by Heckel, Biebrich
(photograph kindly supplied by Edith Reiter, Biebrich).

The modern instrument (Pl 6) stands about 134cm tall. In total length its bore measures about 254cm and flares from a width of ca 4mm at the tip of the crook to ca 39mm across the end of the bell. While Almenräder's 1843 chart gave a chromatic range of four octaves (B♭′ to b♭″), the standard compass today extends to e″ or f″ (even higher notes may are sometimes called for but these require unauthodox techniques, such as biting the reed, to obtain them).

The bassoon consists of four joints made of wood, a metal crook (or bocal) and a reed:

- The crook or bocal, on which the reed is fitted, is inserted into the top of the tenor joint. It is a conical tube of German silver, an alloy of nickel, zinc and copper, unplated or plated with either nickel or silver – although other alloys (brass in particular) and platings (gold) are sometimes used. A pin-hole at the wider end is protected by a protruding nipple. It is bent into a characteristic curve, although the shape is occasionally modified to suit individual players. They are supplied in different lengths (see §3.2).
- The 'wing' is so called after the protruding shoulder, which accommodates the obliquely drilled finger-holes. It is lined with vulcanized rubber – or some similiar synthetic compound. The smooth innner surface of the lining not only protects against water damage but is considered to be acoustically beneficial.
- The butt joint (boot joint, double joint) is fitted at the base with a detachable metal U-bend bow, which is protected by a butt-cap. The descending bore is usually lined – and sometimes the ascending one as well.
- The long or bass joint, which lies adjacent to the wing joint.
- The bell joint is tipped with an ornamental rim. In former times this was a traditional ring of ivory, but today it is most often made of a synthetic substitute; alternatively a metal band, similar to that on French models, is fitted. Its exterior bulbous profile is decorative. An alternative extended bell designed for low A′ is sometimes used (see §3.2 *Extras*).

The wood used for the German instrument is sycamore maple (*Acer pseudoplatanus*). The American maker Fox also uses local sugar maple (*Acer saccharum*), as well as the synthetic polypropylene. In order to achieve the necessary stability, the wood needs to be thoroughly seasoned and then machined in gradual stages. Sometimes the wood is specially treated in order to hasten the process of stabilization. The machining of the bore and tone-holes calls for a high degree of precision, while the final tuning must be done by hand – a delicate and time consuming process. Factors such as these contribute to the high cost of the bassoon compared with that of other woodwind intruments.

For recent refinements and improvements adopted in recent years see §3.2 *Extras*.

§2.2 The French *basson*

Description

The French model of bassoon, popularly known as the 'Buffet' after the well-known Paris maker Buffet-Crampon, differs in many respects from the German model. Its key-system (Pl 7) reflects a disposition of tone-holes that still retains much in common with the early bassoon. Rather than maple, palissander palissander/rosewood (various *Dalbergia* species) has been the preferred wood; being more dense and when combined with a slightly narrower bore it gives the French instrument a brighter sound. The upward range extends to f″ without undue difficulty. Compared with the *Fagott*, the upper register responds more freely; consequently certain artistic effects are easier to realize. The reed style, especially in France, has traditionally had a so-called chisel scrape (see §3.3); however where both *basson* and *Fagott* used happily to   co-exist – such as New

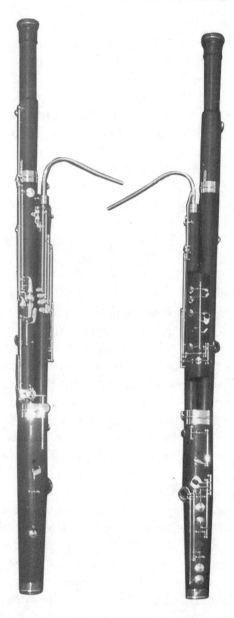

Plate 7
Modern *basson* by Buffet-Crampon
(photograph by Dominic Weir, London).

The Bassoon

York in the 1930s and London from the 1930s to 1960s – players sometimes adopted the 'German' type of reed – scraped with thinned tip and edges around a central spine or heart – in order to render their sound more compatible. From the 1970s efforts have been made to defend its status in France. Maurice Allard collaborated with Buffet-Crampon in 1975 to develop an improved model of instrument and crook. He also founded the pressure group *les Amis du basson français*, (active 1975-1983). The Selmer company also brought out an alternative model, which has been preferred by some on account of its free responsiveness.

Use

Up until the 1930s both French bassoon and French horn were in standard use in England. After that time both instruments began to be replaced by German models of which many mourned the loss of the French tone-colours; they perceived them as being more truly characteristic of these instruments – in those early days the *Fagott* could hardly rival the *basson* in terms of expressiveness. In recent years a number of professional players have felt the *basson* to be a more authentic vehicle for the performance of French repertoire than the *Fagott*. In the 1970s Maurice Allard accepted in his Paris Conservatoire class a few foreign *Fagott* players anxious to train on the French instrument. One of these was Gerald Corey (at that time in Baltimore, now in Ottawa), who has since pioneered the use professionally of both *basson* and *Fagott* for their respective repertoires. Those bassoonists raised on the *Fagott*, who may feel curious about an instrument boasting so many accomplished artists today, will find the *basson* a fascinating challenge that will reveal much about the way French composers have traditionally used the instrument.

Effects such as staccato and vibrato are especially suited to it and can be achieved with comparative ease.

Playing technique

For the player of the *Fagott*, it is the number of new fingerings he must learn that will be a major hurdle. By comparison a larger vocabulary of alternative fingerings is required to humour the often uneven scale. Allard's tutor (Allard, 1975) gives a pair of charts, differentiating between those fingerings used *pour le technique* – which are comparatively simple – and *pour la sonorité* – which are more complicated. There is also less homogeneity between the different notes and registers. The *Fagott*, long considered the 'safer' of the two instruments – though condescendingly termed the 'mumblephone' by the last master of the *basson* in London Cecil James (1913-99) – has gained ground over the *basson* to the extent that the two are now considered by some to be complementary instruments. *Vive la différence!*

§2.3   The Double Bassoon (Contrabassoon)

Description

The modern double bassoon (or contra) (Pl 8) is built one octave lower than the standard bassoon, with a normal range from B♭″ to c′. It is a transposing instrument, notated one octave higher than it sounds. The modern 'compact' model stands about 122cm tall. Earlier models had a tall down-turning bell, which had two advantages: the body, being less wide, allowed for better visibility, and a shorter 'C bell' could be substituted when, as is often the case, low B♮″ and B♭″ were not required. Models descending to A″

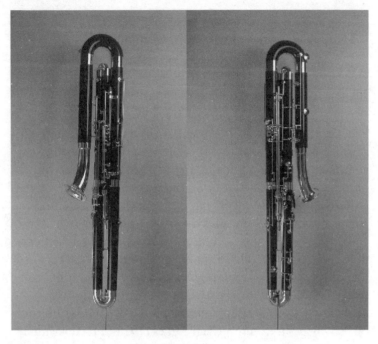

Plate 8
Modern *Kontrafagott* by Heckel, Biebrich
(photograph kindly supplied by Edith Reiter, Biebrich).

require that the basic bore-length of 5.5m is extended by means of a longer bell. Most players hold the instrument between their legs, supporting it on the ground with an adjustable end-pin. The reed is somewhat larger than that of the bassoon. The crook is inserted into a metal shank incorporating tuning-slide and water-key.

History

The baroque *Kontrafagott*, like the *Grossbassdulzian*, was in its construction essentially an enlarged version of the normal 8′ model. Herbert Heyde has pointed out that the latter, while expensive to build, justified its cost, since it could produce as much sound as three players of the string bass. A surviving 4-key English contra descending to B♭″ by Thomas Stanesby (London 1739) stands 253cm high. However comparatively few later 18th century instruments extended below C′ (or D′). Scores by Haydn (*The Creation*) and Beethoven (9th Symphony) calling for low B♭″ relied on the player's ingenuity rather than keywork. Mozart's *Maurerische Trauermusik* (K477) descends to C′. In the first half of the 19th century 6-keyed contra models were produced in Austria and Bohemia, but the lack of satisfactory instruments elsewhere prevented its employment outside these countries. Wide-bore instruments such as Haseneier's *Contrabassophon* (1847), Červeny's *Tritonicon* (1856) and Mahillon's *contrebasse à anche* (1868) were developed for band use, but at the time were considered unsatisfactory in the orchestra. In 1879 Heckel's foreman Stritter produced the first true modern contra, held like a bassoon but with its bore folded several times to make it compact. It is on this that all subsequent contra models have been based. Efforts that have been long overdue are at last being made currently in both Germany and the US to rectify long-standing problems concerning the placement of the harmonic-key tone-holes. Meanwhile the *Contraforte* (2001), an innovative model with a wider bore by Guntram Wolf (Kronach) claiming to deliver enhanced power without loss of tone-character, has been well received.

In late 19th century France only the metal *sarrusophone contrebasse en ut* (family first patented by Gautrot in 1856), was available until Buffet introduced their *contrebasson* with French-system keywork in 1906. However it would be a mistake to suppose that works such as Ravel's *l'Heure espagnole* and Dukas' *l'Apprenti sorcier* that call for the greater strength of the wider-bored instrument might better have been played on the *contrebasson*.

The Bassoon

In Performance

While the upper register is relatively weak, it is in the middle and lower register that the contra comes into its own. The challenge for the player is to produce a tone sufficiently weighty to 'tell' in *tutti* without forfeiting quality and flexibility. Its fingering is similar to that of the bassoon, except in the upper register where, due in part to the instrument's relative lack of development (see above), the player must be prepared to experiment with fingerings somewhat more than on bassoon. Instead of a single open-standing crook-key as on the bassoon, there are the equivalent of two, which remain closed until activated. The main problem lies in the enhanced demands on the breath, both in terms of quantity and quality. The instrument should not be approached as an extension of the low register of the bassoon, but pitched with a comparable degree of accuracy in its middle register. If and when we can succeed in meeting these demands we will find that our bassoon-playing has benefitted. The dimensions of the reed that can best satisfy requirements may vary from player to player; while some look essentially like larger bassoon reeds, with others the blade may be proportionately longer.

To achieve an efficient playing position on the contra, we will need to adopt one different from that used on bassoon. When considering what this might be, it is vital to avoid any problems that might impair comfort and prejudice the increased demand for air. The considerable width of the instrument can make seeing the conductor difficult, while the use of a spike might impose certain limitations. By trying such experiments as:

- altering the chair angle
- rotating the crook
- altering the angle of instrument and the height of spike
- altering the bend of the crook

a position might be found that presents the reed to the mouth at a favourable angle without requiring the trunk to be twisted or contorted. We should hold the instrument in front of us, just sufficiently left of centre, to allow for music and conductor to be visible. Any adjustment needed to read the music should be made with eyes and music stand, rather than by turning of the head.

Repertoire and Use

The contra fulfils a vital role in the orchestra by giving fundamental support in the contrabass register to the entire wind section. Brahms specified its use in his *Ein Deutsches Requiem* whenever the organ might be lacking. The technical demands made by the majority of 19th century orchestral parts are refreshingly modest. In certain works such as Beethoven's 9th Symphony it is asked to double the florid passage-work given to the cellos and basses, but this is probably due to absentmindedness (although he had taken the trouble in his 4th and 6th Symphonies to simplify certain cello passages for the double bass). Wagner, who had refrained from using the instrument hitherto, endorsed Heckel's new model after it was demonstrated to him in Bayreuth in 1877 by subsequently employing it in *Parsifal* (1883). Thenceforth it has been adopted as a regular member of the woodwind family, a natural and irreplaceable complement to the bassoon section. Some 20th century scores make exacting technical demands, requiring it to be no less agile than the bassoon (Schoenberg's *Kammersymphonie* op. 9, Berg's *Kammerkonzert* etc.). Perhaps the best use of the contra is in subtle writing where it can be heard soloistically – such as in Schoenberg's *Gurrelieder* (which calls for a pair) or Dohnányi's *Nursery Variations*. In many cases the same player is required to double on both bassoon and contra (the rapid alternating between the two is a manoeuvre calling for some dexterity). Formerly the task of the 3rd or 4th player of the section, works are increasing being scored for a single player required to double on both instruments. In recent years it has appeared as a concert soloist (see §6.2).

§2.4 Playing 'period' Bassoons

Modern versions of such instruments as dulcian (curtal), baroque bassoon and classical bassoon that their makers claim to have been copied from identified originals have been on the market for some years. They have found a ready market among the professional, university student and amateur wishing to play early music on early instruments. The market for 'historically informed' performance has enjoyed a remarkable growth in recent years – with specialist period groups annexing much of the former repertoire of the symphony orchestra.

Several printed sources are currently available that give practical tips on how to get started on such instruments (see §6.1). As in the case of the contra, the bassoonist can derive much value from 'having a go' on such instruments. Apart from the fun of grappling with the challenges, many of the skills learned in the process can be used later on the modern instrument. These benefits include:

- being taught to place greater reliance on breath and embouchure control, rather than the use of the crook-and harmonic-keys
- having learned the original fingerings that simplify so many fingering problems, making many of them work on the modern instrument
- coping with differing models of reed, which teaches embouchure skills and stamina.

In our search for the chimera of ultimate 'authenticity', the following points should be borne in mind:

- In order to build a trustworthy replica, it is not enough for the maker merely to have taken accurate measurements; he needs to have had considerable experience with playing original instruments in general and his chosen model in particular. Museums are not always willing these days to grant such facilities.
- not all of today's 'copies' conform with any degree of accuracy to their originals
- surviving instruments have often suffered deterioration and intervention; even when unaltered, their dimensions will differ minutely from when they were made
- A modern billet of wood – however treated – behaves and responds differently compared with the wood of an original 18th century bassoon; resonance and responsiveness are among the factors that are critically affected. It is arguable however that 18th century billets, when new, might not have been so different (!).
- although the crook plays a crucial role in determining such matters as pitch, fingering and response, virtually no originals survive together with their associated instruments
- The reed is another accessory about which the same can be said; the modern-type of reed used by many of today's practitioners produces a tone hardly corresponding to the characteristic sound described in early writings. Such reeds often preclude the use of the basic fingerings given in charts. It is significant that, with a reed whose proportions, gouge and binding reflect early reed-making practice (see §1 *Baroque*), then such problems largely disappear. Although significant research regarding early reeds has been carried out in recent times, the findings have largely yet to be utilised.

Three
The Instrument

§3.1 Choice of Model

New

There is at present a wide variety of choice to be made between makers from such countries as Germany, the Czech Republic, the UK, the US and Japan. Trade fairs attended by the leading makers, such as those organised periodically by national Double Reed societies, offer an ideal opportunity for the prospective buyer to try out and compare models and prices. Those factories that turn out instruments in quantity will have available for instant delivery a range of different models; smaller workshops that make to personal order will usually have a long waiting list.

Many makers are anxious to promote the addition of such extras as additional keywork, finger-hole tubes, rollers, keywork in silver; while such extras might appear to justify a higher asking price, it should be borne in mind that:

- each added tone-hole will augment the volume of the bore by that of its 'chimney'; an affecting of acoustic thereby cannot be ruled out
- every protruding finger-hole tube, every added tone-hole, will create extra air-stream turbulence, which can add to resistance

- plating: resistence to the tarnishing effects of acidic sweat may be a consideration here (apart from the aesthetics). Silver plating has a 'soapy' smooth feel, which for some people obviates the need for rollers; nickel-plating, often used on less expensive instruments, is preferred by many for its resistance to tarnish.
- solid silver keywork, which is considerably more expensive, is heavier and prone to tarnish.

Some bassoons these days are made of plastic rather than wood, which are built by the US maker Fox, now the world's largest producer of double-reed instruments. Among their advantages are:

- Consistency: wood being a natural material is subject to considerable variation over which the maker has little influence and is unable to detect until the instrument is largely finished. In comparison, plastic can be manu-factured under very close tolerances. The resulting instruments are therefore very much more consistent.
- Durability: plastic is not subject to cracking and stands up well to hard use.

Among the disadvantages offered by plastic are:

- Condensation: because of the surface properties of plastic it is possible for condensation to occur more readily, which can lead more readily to water-logged tone-holes.
- Weight and feel: compared with wood, plastic is a denser material; instruments are therefore somewhat heavier. Plastic has different heat conduction properties and can feel, at least initially, colder to the touch.

Every new instrument will require a period of 'blowing-in'. As was necessary in former times with the running-in of a new car, special care should be exercised during the initial months to follow the makers' instructions.

Secondhand

Secondhand instruments offer a number of advantages:

- being already blown-in, they will remain more stable in their response
- the wood by now is well matured, and thus less liable to crack
- pre-war bassoons are lighter in weight and, being slimmer in girth, easier to play for those with small hands; they are often easier to blow, offering less resistance
- pre-war instruments are considered by many to be superior tonally to those made post-war, though their flatter pitch of A = 435/437.5Hz has to be coped with; pre-war Heckel crooks, which were built of special alloys, are particularly sought after.

Disadvantages to watch out for include:

- wood rot at the bottom of the unlined bore of the butt just above the U-bend bow; note however that this is a problem that the repairman can usually solve
- gross interventions, especially if carried out to the finger-holes
- poor tuning of the basic scale
- basic pitch (see below)
- while minor cracks in the tenons can be tolerated, those in the body itself are potentially much more serious
- a joint that does not correspond with the others – i.e. that is an unsigned replacement
- damage to crook.

Note that general response can be adversely affected by an unsuitable crook, or a high 'leak factor' (i.e. poor sealing by pads).

Investing in a used bassoon involves a not inconsiderable sum of money; as with a car, it makes sense to engage an expert to carry out an unbiased appraisal. It should be noted that instruments made post-war in Eastern Europe and China can vary very considerably in quality.

The following maxim is worth remembering for anyone wishing to upgrade from an inferior instrument: we will instinctively give preference to the instrument that most closely resembles our old one, rather than to one that does not; but paradoxically this is the very type with which we are dissatisfied and wish to replace. A better strategy would be to find an instrument whose excellence can be vouched for – such as one that a player whom we trust is selling for legitimate reasons – and buy it, whatever our initial impression might be. We should be confident that, after the necessary apprenticeship period learning how to respond to it, we will be better served.

The Heckelfagott

The reputation enjoyed worldwide by Heckel bassoons (made in Biebrich near Wiesbaden since 1831) has remained a unique phenomenon for most of the last century. Although in London such leading players as Archie Camden and Gwydion Brooke patronised their Saxon rivals Oscar Adler (who had opened a Manchester agency in the 1920s), elsewhere the *Heckelfagott* has long been the preferred instrument, occupying pride of place amongst professional and amateur worldwide (their trade links with the UK go back to the 1851 London exhibition). This dominant position has become somewhat eroded in recent decades, partly because of their refusal to enlarge their manufacturing capacity, and because of the ever increasing competitiveness in quality, price, and delivery time on the part of other manufacturers. However, while some early Heckel instruments are hardly worth resuscitating, a very large number indeed continue to give unrivalled service throughout the world to their proud owners. Good 7000 and 8000 series bassoons are especially sought after internationally by professionals, while those from the 4000 and 5000 series are still sweet-toned and responsive to play, if somewhat lacking in projection*. While it can hardly be said that every post-war Heckel series has inevitably improved on its predecessors, both their current bassoon and contra models (i.e. those dating from around 2000) are considered by many to be superior to anything produced in the past.

Heckel bassoons have undergone a certain evolution over the years. Earlier instruments were characterized by having longer bores and indeed Alan Fox, who has modelled his own instruments on this characteristic, differentiates between what his company terms their 'long bore' and 'short bore' models as follows:

- the long bore model was the model Heckel built from prior to World War I until the mid 1920s – ie pre 6000 series instruments only
- The 'short bore' model, about an inch shorter, "is a more common instrument, being Heckel's primary production effort between the mid 1920s and the late 1950s, and being the design of every commercially built bassoon that has used Heckel as a pattern instrument. [...] The tone of the short-bore bassoon is brighter than that of the other; and with proper bore design (or

* Heckel serial numbers: pre 1877 unnumbered; 3000 = 1877; 4000 = 1898; 5000 = 1911; 6000 = 1924; 7000 = 1929; 8000 = 1936; 9000 = 1943; 10,000 = 1956; 11,000 = 1965; 12,000 = 1975; 13,000 = 1985.

help from the player's reed) the sound 'carries an edge' which penetrates throughout the largest concert halls" (Fox, 1968).

Pitch

In spite of the international treaty of 1939 establishing pitch at A = 440 Hz, which was re-ratified after the War, many countries nowadays deviate from this standard. Although seldom publicized, it is a fact that all Japanese instruments are now made to A = 442 Hz, while orchestras in Berlin and Vienna (where there is a long tradition of playing sharper than elsewhere) tune cold to around A = 446 Hz. This has obvious implications for the pitch of instruments made for the domestic market in these countries.

In the UK 'sharp' or 'philharmonic' pitch (A = 451 Hz) was in general use for civilian music-making until the early 20th century, by the military until World War II and by brass bands until even later. There are still many bassoons in existence that were built to this pitch – including both English-made French-system *bassons* and genuine *Heckelfagotte*; these are strictly collectors' items only.

§3.2 Crook, Accessories, Extras, Modifications

While a new instrument leaves the maker's workshop nominally ready to pick up and play, over a period of time most players will need to customize his or her own instrument in order to make it better suit them.

The Bassoon

Crook (Bocal)

This is a component that can exercise the greatest effect on the acoustics of the entire instrument (see also §4.8 *Acoustics*). It is apparent that the crook is able to match, or mediate between, the style of reed a player prefers to use with the acoustic needs of the instrument; for this reason players often retain their old crook when switching to a different instrument. Like the violinist searching for a perfect bow, the bassoonist may have to expend much time and effort in selecting a crook before he is satisfied.

The crook is made by wrapping a shaped piece of sheet metal around a long mandrel. After annealing and soldering of the seam the tube is filled with a special low-melting-point metal. The crook is then bent to the manufacturer's desired shape – the low-melting-point metal ensures that the tube will not collapse while bending. After bending this metal is removed by immersing the crook in hot water. If we wish later to alter the angle or curvature of a crook we should apply the same technique, of infilling with a low-melting-point metal, that was used during manufacture rather than attempting to bend it without taking such a precaution (see §7.3 *Appendix III*).

Crooks are manufactured to various specifications of length, bore, wall-thickness and wall-material. These are designed to favour different aspects of playing, such as high register, resistance, pitch etc. Crooks are often identified by a number to denote length, and letters to denote bore and material. It is an unfortunate fact that the mandrels on which different makes of crook are made are neither standardised in diameter nor taper; nor is there any standardisation between manufacturers in designation. In consequence the testing of alternative crooks can become a tiresome process and one that is highly subjective. To achieve any form of objectivity it is necessary to test a new crook in the acoustic conditions of a performance and to

32

enlist the help of others to listen from some distance, especially when making comparisons.

Popkin & Glickman propose the following 'quality testing' routine for crooks; this is to listen for undesirable changes in tone-quality, pitch and resistance whilst playing at ♩ = 60 the notes c, d, e, e′ without altering the embouchure (Popkin & Glickman, 1987).

Standard pin-hole diameters were first enlarged by the innovative repairman Hans Moennig (1903-1988, *fl.* Philadelphia) in order to facilitate the speech of the upper octave (Fr.: *octavation*); 0.6mm to 0.8mm is common these days.

To ensure a perfect seal between reed and crook, it is good to whip the end with a lapping of fine greased thread.

During the course of playing, we need to remove and replace the crook frequently to remove condensation, while requiring it to stay firmly in place at other times. A lapping of thicker waxed thread overlaid on top with that of finer gauge serves well for this purpose – and is preferable to cork.

Support Systems

Of the many alternative methods of supporting the instrument today, there is not one that is ideal; each will be found to offer advantages and disadvantages. The bassoon of today is unfortunately heavier than ever before; even a pre-World War II bassoon weighs less than its present-day counterpart, while period bassooons are light enough to need hardly any supporting apparatus. In deciding which system to adopt, it is important to consider the resulting position of instrument in relation to body. This will have implications not only for arms and shoulders – whether weight is distributed evenly – but (more importantly) for reed-angle at the lips; it may be dangerous to switch continually between different systems if this is grossly affected.

The Bassoon

Comparative pros and cons for six systems of support are considered below. With systems **1** and **2** – neck-strap and harness – the instrument lies close to the body, touching the right thigh, and is attached by means of the eyelet-ring on the upper butt-joint mount – a method going back well over two centuries. It is often beneficial to fit an extension ('balance-hanger') to this in order for it to hang closer to the bassoon's point of balance, and thus distribute its weight more evenly between the two arms. The other systems **3** to **6** each impose differing restrictions on free body movement.

1 Neck-Strap (Sling)
pro
- close contact is enjoyed between player and instrument, permitting considerable freedom of movement

con
- in time the weight of the instrument can cause discomfort, especially around the back of the neck – although this can be mitigated by using a broad width of strap
- this resultant weight can pull the neck forward

2 Harness
pro
- the weight of a heavy instrument is evenly distributed between neck and shoulders

con
- the webbing straps can constrain the upper chest

3 Seat-Strap
especially popular in the US, this requires an eyelet-ring or perforation on the under-side of the butt-cap, through which to hook the end of the strap

pro
- zero weight around the neck or shoulders
- it enables the instrument to be held further away from the body, if desired

con
- it can impose a vastly disproportionate weight on the left forearm, causing possible tendon strain
- it cannot be used whilst standing

4 Leg-Rest
developed and marketed in Holland, and popular in that country; employs a universal coupling (which can be locked) attached to a collar fixed around the upper butt mount

pro
- as with **3**, it enables the instrument to be held further away from the body
- once adjusted, neither weight around neck and shoulders, nor any pressure on arms, wrists or hands

con
- it cannot be used standing up

5 Floor Stand
pro
- Compared with the heavy floor-stand to which the instrument might be clamped, made back in the 1950s by the Heckel company, the design recently developed by John Orford (London) is vastly improved. Adaptable for either sitting or standing, it offers the player 100% freedom by featuring two universal couplings, one at floor level resting on a low tripod, the other attached to a collar around the upper butt mount. A similar device employing a low tripod and single coupling invented by Maarten Vonk (NL-Amersfoort) grips directly onto the butt-cap.

The Bassoon

con
- the player is constrained to one fixed location; some might consider this to cramp style whilst standing
- some may require alterations to the case to accommodate the modifications to the instrument

6 Spike (End-Pin)
commonly used for playing the contra, it requires a collar to be brazed on to the butt-cap to accept the spike; the end should be fitted with a non-slip rubber tip
pro
- resting the instrument against the right shank results in zero weight around the neck, nor any pressure on arms, wrists or hands
- when not playing, the instrument can remain in quasi vertical position, rather than being constantly raised and lowered, thus obviating problems with water in the finger-holes
- once the height of the spike has been correctly adjusted, this will serve to maintain a good playing position indefinitely
- both sitting or standing to play is possible; for the latter, it may be rested on a chair

con
- modifying of the shape of crook will often be necessary
- it places a strain on the metal housing at the foot of the butt joint; this can cause the housing to become loosened thereby introducing an air leak
- it may require modifications to the case to accommodate the modifications to the butt-cap.

Hand-Rest (Crutch)

It is customary to fit a hand-rest on the butt – though its use is comparatively infrequent in the US. It should lend support to assist the fingers in the execution of technical passages (see §4.7 *Application*); it can also give the player a more secure grasp of the instrument. Each player's individual hand will, according to its shape and size, have differing requirements in order to achieve this. Those designs which engage with the web between the thumb and forefinger often hamper mobility and freedom of the fingers.

The author made his own hand-rest by first modelling in 'plasticine' (a type of malleable clay) a hand-rest moulded to offer support to that part of the hand just below the bottom phalanges of the three middle fingers, but without interfering elsewhere; this he then carved in wood. Others have used a resin, similar to that used for car body-work repairs, by filling a small plastic bag with the soft resin and grasping this in the right hand until the resin begins to harden; once hardened the bag is peeled away and the resin smoothed using an abrasive paper.

Case

The designs of case have altered over the years. Common in 19th century France was an upright octagonal 'stove-pipe' case in wood, lined in padded leather. In England a similar model, shaped either square or cylindrical in massive leather, was the norm, especially for military instruments. German instruments have been regularly supplied with a type like a suitcase. With the availability of modern light-weight fabrics and insulation materials the 'gig-bag' model, which can be worn like a rucksack, has now become deservedly popular.

The Bassoon

Extras

Not all of those listed below – that many makers are understandably keen to promote – are indispensable in the long term:

- rollers; they can facilitate the sliding of finger from key to key, although sensitive control may be forfeited
- certain finger-holes and tone-holes bushed with metal tubes (developed by Hans Moennig in the the mid 1920s) to prevent the entry of moisture; only worth contemplating if the support system in use provokes water problems. Note that any such protrusions in the bore may create extra resistance. There are also other less invasive solutions to this problem, which should be attempted first; the use of a piece of string soaked in linseed oil and drawn through the bore avoiding tone holes can be highly effective in forming a track on which moisture condenses.
- lining both of the butt bores
- improving the sealing quality (i.e. reducing the 'leak factor') by treating skin pads with paraffin wax, while replacing others with cork instead – another of Moennig's innovations (but see §3.4 *'leak factor'*)
- high d″ key for left-hand thumb: hardly indispensable, although almost standard today
- keys for high e″, high f″ (adopted into the Buffet system for several decades)
- an automatic venting mechanism on the wing-joint devised in 2001 by Arthur Weisberg (Boca Raton, Florida) to obviate the need to 'flick' (see §4.8 *Fingering*)
- alternative crook-key for left-hand little finger, mounted on the wing-joint, the touch lying below the low E♭ and C♯ keys (thus requiring a degree of finger-stretch); this is extremely useful [a] in freeing the left-hand thumb for other duties, [b] obviating need to operate

the crook-lock, [c] improving speech of middle a, b♭, b♮ and c′ by permitting closure of the crook pin-hole whilst operating the harmonic keys (this was the standard location for the crook key in the Buffet system – the thumb key being a later addition)

- A♭-B♭ trill mechanism: hardly indispensable
- extra low C touch (spatula) for left-hand thumb: either a help or a hindrance, according to individual left-hand thumb technique (see §4.7 *Application*)
- 'whisper-key' locking device (crook-lock): variant designs for either thumb are available – mostly unnecessary when the alternate crook key is available
- a modification carried out to the long and bell joints, whereby part of the former is permanently built on to the latter so that the instrument fits into a smaller case (the 'gentleman' or compact model)
- mute: two basic types are known:
  - **a** a brass cylinder inserted into two-thirds of the bell, six to eight centimetres long lined with felt, with the end covered with gauze – advocated by the conductor Hermann Scherchen (Scherchen, 1927)
  - **b** a metal disc operating like the butterfly-valve of a carburettor built into the long joint ca 80mm above the D tone-hole – described by Yuri Neklyudov (Neklyudov, 1966)
- low A′ bell – note that this can affect the intonation and response of the middle and upper registers
- low C♯/D♯ trill mechanism – practically impossible to execute without this; the very simple and effective addition of a touch to the C♯ rod that is positioned to the left of the low C touch.

The Bassoon

Modifications

- 'short-reach' model bassoon; some finger-holes covered etc, designed for players with small hands
- left-hand-rest: the spot on the instrument where the base joint of the left-hand index finger rests is built up with a curved shaped layer of cork
- adjusting the relative heights of the touches of the left-hand thumb keys on the wing to enable the thumb to shift from one to the other without hitting those in between.

For details of the modifications carried out by the author to his own instrument, see §7.2 *Appendix II*.

§3.3   The Reed

As with §3.4 *Maintenance*, it lies outside the scope of this book to provide detailed instructions on reed-making given the amount of authoritative literature currently available (see §6.1 *Bibliography*).

Cane

Reed-cane (*Arundo donax*) may be aptly described as a bilaminate of two substances, each of which reacts differently to water. As with the skin of an orange, an impermeable rind is bonded to a layer of pith, the density of whose texture becomes progressively less according to depth. The higher proportion of vascular (capillary) bundles to pith just below the bark gives a texture of greater density and resilience than that found at deeper levels. In recent years ground-breaking research has been carried out by Dr Jean-Marie Heinrich (F-Mulhouse) into cane and its relevance to the bassoon-reed, including the variability and significance of its density. Since 1998 he has been working with the Munich reed-maker Ricardo Döringer, and their professional collaboration promises much for the future.*

Among the variable features in a given piece of cane may be:

- its provenance – whether from France, Russia, the Americas, China etc
- whether harvested in spring or in autumn
- the time-length and method of seasoning by grower
- the length of retention by reed-maker prior to making up
- the effective degree of hardness; different degrees of hardness may suit different kinds of reed
- the straightness of grain
- the degree of density – which can vary from tube to tube, and even from one part to another of the same tube.

Stock

In the late 17th century reeds were built on a staple (similar to that of the oboe), a method still in local use up to the mid 19th century. It can be shown to offer such advantages as the greater degree of blade flexibility desirable for a baroque-style reed. In the 1890s the Parisian reed-maker Rabut produced a commercial model where the blade ends were inserted into a solid metal sheath (Pl 9c). The Moscow bassoonist Yuri Neklyudov (*b* 1918) has designed a metal staple, turned thicker at the base and chamfered at the top, around which the ends of the blades are wired, claiming that this method increased the stability, consistency and longevity of his reeds (Neklyudov, 1966).

* The *Pro Reeds* company, based in Munich.

The Bassoon

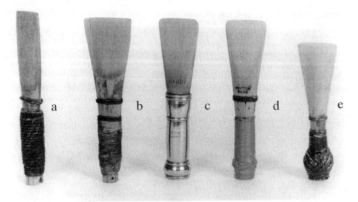

Plate 9
Historic bassoon reeds (author's collection)
a signed by Thomas Ling (*d* London 1853), documented from 1794 as
bassoonist, from 1823 as reed-maker; slightly rotated to reveal
characteristic 'swallow-tail' stock; note soldered ring around throat
b signed by Joseph Witton, *fl*. London 1840s
c signed 'Rabut', 'Rabut deposé', Paris ca1890; stock encased in
nickel-silver sheath
d signed 'Prosper Colas', Paris ca1885
e by Kurt Ludwig, Munich early 1960s.

Banding

The adding of wire to binding thread, which offers a useful
means of reed adjustment denied to the oboist, was first
documented in the mid 17th century. An alternative
method, adopted by early 19th century English reed-
makers, was to fit a loose fitting soldered metal band which
could be shifted to alter blade tension (Pl 9a). Of the three
bands of wire used on modern reeds, each of which serves a
different function, the top band (nearest to the blade) needs
to be comparatively loose, so that it may act as a fulcrum.

*Gouge**

The first to mechanize the gouging process was the French oboist Henri Brod (1799-1839), who invented a flat-bed machine for oboe reeds in 1834 that planed to a rigidly parallel gouge, the same principle on which most modern hand-operated machines work. The effect of this on bassoon reeds is that gouging to the minimum thickness of cane sufficient for the stock will leave it too thick at the tip; thus when made up, the better-quality rind-wood towards the tip has to be removed, exposing coarser-grained pith-wood.

In contradiction to this, all early reed-making sources agree that, when gouging by hand with a scoop-shaped chisel, the piece was to be left thinner towards the centre (i.e. midway between the two extremities), a process demanding time and care. When made up, so little thinning of the blade would be required that it was hardly considered necessary to describe the process – in marked contrast to the practices of today. In modern times Lou Skinner devised a set of scraping-wheel hand-tools to facilitate this operation (McKay, 2000). It was thanks to the durable qualities of this rind-wood at the tip that Carl Almenräder could in 1829 claim a life-span of up to two years for a reed in daily use (Almenräder, 1829).

Mechanization

In recent years the reed-making process has been further mechanized. The Los Angeles bassoonist Don Christlieb (1912-2001) pioneered the use of the micrometer from the late 1940s, designing machinery to undertake many of the processes. The *Aussenhobelmaschine* (profiler) and

---

* gouge: the process of removing cane from the inside of the piece

The Bassoon

Anspitzhobelmaschine (tip profiler) were developed later in Germany by Kunibert Michel (Hanover) and Georg Rieger (Gaggenau) and have been copied elsewhere. A significant advance was made when diamond-tipped high-speed cutting techniques were introduced that permitted profiling uphill (i.e. against the grain). In recent years Paul Buttemer (Victoria, BC) and Ricardo Döringer (Munich) have each developed computer-steered machines able to reproduce a profile entered digitally.

Design and Manufacture

The reed in general use today has a blade scraped with thinned tip and edges around a central spine or heart; this 'German' type contrasts with the 'French' type of reed that has traditionally had a chisel scrape.

As with oboe reeds there is a considerable degree of divergence of opinion regarding both the manufacture and specification of dimension and profile of bassoon reeds in use today. The reeds produced by the legendary reed-maker Kurt Ludwig (1892-1967, *fl.* Munich ca1930-67) (Pl 10) enjoyed an international reputation. Having first met him in 1952 the author enjoyed the privilege of using his reeds for 50 years. What follows is an attempt to document key features of his work – design, preparation and finishing – by comparing them point by point with current practice.

Today's average machine-produced reed will usually show the following characteristics:

1   a longitudinal inner gouge that is parallel
2   a shape machined to a consistent specification
3   a rather modest thickness of wood at the stock
4   almost cylindrical in shape at the middle wire
5   a top band of wire that is no less tight than the others, thus exercising considerable pressure on the blades

Plate 10
Reed-maker Kurt Ludwig (*b* Dresden 1892; *d* Munich 1967),
bassoonist, contrabassoonist and professional reed-maker active in
Munich from before 1932.

6   a scrape machined with a 'profiler' to carefully pre-calcu-
lated thicknesses

7   considerable rigidity at the back of the blade compared to
the front, contributing to a comparatively low level of
responsiveness

8   each blade-flank of identical dimension

9   no traces of bark remaining on the blade

10   a texture of cane at the tip that tends to be coarse rather than fine, thus affecting its resulting thickness at the tip and shape at the aperture; it should be noted that if the piece of cane has been gouged to show a crescent-moon-shaped lateral profile – that is, thinner at the sides and thicker in the middle – this will affect the quality of cane at either side of the tip

11   relatively little selection of raw material exercised

12   built over a short and concentrated period of working time.

By contrast the reeds of Kurt Ludwig displayed the following features (Pl 9e):

1   his gouging machine produced (in two stages) an inner gouge sloping from 1.4mm thick at each extremity to 0.9mm thin in the middle; further convex thinning was carried out by hand

2   being shaped by hand (guided by eye), the specification could be modified to suit the individual client

3   considerable thickness of wood (1.4mm) at the stock to lend stability

4   a middle band of wire using a thinner gauge, thrice-wrapped, that has already become oval, rather than cylindrical, in shape

5   a top band of wire that is quite oval, tending to looseness, acting as a fulcrum to the blades, allowing them a greater degree of vibration

6   Preparation of the scrape executed by hand, with relative thicknesses determined, according to the properties of the individual piece of cane, by empirical trial rather than predetermined calculation. Once made up, he finished the blades by using a cutting, rather than a scraping, technique. With tongue and mandrel inserted he would hold the reed with the left hand, the tip nearest to him; his knife, with large fat-shaped handle and a small, narrow, thin, pointed and extremely sharp blade, he held in the right. Guided by the thumb and paring upwards, he could remove cane quite quickly in the form of thin slices of wood like fish-scales.

7   all parts of the blade with the capacity to participate in various patterns of vibration

8   with the dimensions of each right-hand blade-flank left thinner for ease of response, the left-hand blade-flank left thicker to guarantee pitch stability

9   traces of bark visible on the blade, especially at sides of tip

10   cane at the tip that is fine texture, that may be scraped thin without losing resilience, giving reeds that tend to be consistent, that have good longevity, and produce a bright sound that is rich in overtones

11   the painstaking examination and testing of raw material in the early stages of making, with the ruthless rejection of the relatively high proportion of pieces deemed unsuitable

12   built slowly over a period of many days – about one week – allowing adequate time for the wood to settle after each stage of manufacture.

Servicing

Both the response and responsiveness of our reeds will show a cycle of change whereby the flexibility of the blades is affected. While the process of calcification that takes place inside the texture of the cane can hardly be arrested, it is possible to forestall the excessive build-up of dental debris that is deposited whilst we play by the saliva on both the inside and outside of the blades. We need to remove this at periodic intervals.

At early stages this deposit appears to benefit the quality of our tone by filtering out elements of noise. However if allowed to build up too much this will act as a ballast increasing the threshold of resistance – as well as raising issues of hygiene. But when, too much having accumulated, this is removed all at once, the subjective effect can be severe. A treatment that is 'little and often' will be found to serve best. Several methods may be used to remove it:

- using a pipe-cleaner introduced through the stock end, and a sheet of absorbent paper between the blades.
- holding the reed upside down under a cold-water tap and directing a jet of water through
- soaking it in water with a cleansing agent added
- immersing it in a vessel of water wired for ultra-sound that generates microscopic bubbles that carry out a 'scrubbing' action*.

The following system is that favoured by the author:

Interior: carefully introducing a darning needle between the blades to clean away the deposit, restricting attention to those areas that vibrate.

Exterior: inserting a tongue between the blades to guard against splitting and a mandrel into the stock for purchase, wet the blades with saliva and polish with finger wrapped in paper-tissue until they feel clean and smooth to the tongue.

Our kit of essential tools for servicing reeds should include:

- mandrel
- scraping knife
- pair of pliers
- tongue (preferably of ebony or plastic)
- spare pre-cut lengths of wire
- darning needle
- piece of dutch-rush.

§3.4 Maintenance

For detailed instructions an appropriate manual should be consulted (see §6.1 *Bibliography*); what follow are no more than personal hints.

* *Musician's Mate*, trade-marked and available in the US.

In view of the fact that the bassoon is intricate and vulnerable, taking rather little for its correct functioning to be upset, we need:

- to take sensible precautions against mishap
- to be capable of carrying out minor repairs and adjustments ourselves, especially in emergency; to do this we need to keep in our case a basic tool-kit to include screwdriver, lapping thread, joint-grease, oil, as well as reed tools (see §3.3 *Servicing*)
- to have the instrument checked and serviced periodically by a repairman; putting a bassoon into good working order is a job best left to a professional. He will notice and correct incipient problems of which we will be unaware; he will also see that the bore is sufficiently oiled to guard against the wood drying out excessively.

Periodic Servicing

Body

- keep the tenons lubricated with grease; maintain the lapping on the tenons in good order so that, while achieving an adequate air-tight seal, the joints are not too stiff to move
- lapping – of either waxed thread or un-mercerized silk – is superior to cork for the tenon; it is easier to service, less prone to damage, and lends structural strength to the long-joint tenons. "It can be adjusted for thickness when weather changes swell and shrink the wood." (Moennig, 1972)
- keep the tone-holes free of dirt, since particles of fluff from mop or swab can collect in the smaller ones, especially those belonging to the harmonic-keys
- keep the U-bend butt-sump free of any deposit of slime;

49

periodically unscrew, remove and leave open overnight
to allow the entire area to dry out
- clean off any dirt that collects around the keywork with
a small brush.

Crook

- use a special crook pull-through or brush to prevent
any build-up of deposit, which can have a surprising
negative effect on certain high notes
- free the nipple of dirt by poking carefully a piece of
reed-wire through the hole.

Pads

- ensure that their 'leak factor' (see below) is contained
within acceptable limits by having them periodically
checked; the job of treating pad centres with paraffin
wax and their seatings with varnish in order to seal
them is best left to the repairman.

Springs

- ensure that the needle springs function correctly,
becoming activated as required
- keep their action correctly regulated, making a careful
distinction between those that need to be comparatively
stiff and those that might be as light as possible for
comfort
- periodically oil springs to prevent corrosion.

Keywork

- keep all moving parts adequately lubricated. It is
advisable to clean pivots and rods before lubrication;
failure to do so will result in the admixture of dirt and

oil forming an abrasive paste, which ultimately will cause wear; paraffin (kerosene) makes a suitable cleaning agent.

- ensure that the linkage between butt and wing allows the crook-key to operate correctly
- maintain a correct degree of play between the touch of the c″ harmonic key and the c♯ key (both for left thumb) and the mechanism below; the former touch should be further distant than the latter
- ensure that it operates without clatter; if there is noise, identify where and why. Treatment in the short term includes lubricating with thick oil and taking up play by introducing thread between the moving parts; shims cut from sheet-plastic may also be fitted. Longer-term treatment requires special tools and skills and is best left to the repairman.
- check constantly that the 'brille' mechanisms under left-hand ring-finger and right-hand long-finger are not jammed, but functioning correctly
- to avoid tarnish, polish intermittently to remove traces of sweat.

In Use

- avoid violent changes of heat and humidity – for example, unpacking a very cold instrument in a hot room and playing it without having first allowed it to acclimatize
- don't forget to tip out periodically the water that collects in the butt-sump – ideally via the wing socket
- when stowing temporarily on a chair, avoid leaving the instrument so that accumulated water can run into the tone-holes; rest it either on its side edge or with the tone-holes pointing upwards
- when put away in its case after playing, wedging open

the A♭ vent (near the U-bend) with a small piece of cork will allow this vulnerable area of the butt to ventilate properly

- leaving the case open facilitates drying in humid climates: however in drier climates it is better to keep the case closed.

Daily

- Swab out the wing and butt joints after use in order to dry out the bore, using dedicated pull-throughs for each in preference to the traditional mops; for the wing, those made of silk are preferable, this being a lint-free material leaving no residue; for the butt, introduce the spherical ball down the wider socket so as to restrict the moisture to the narrower bore.
- During assembly and disassembly, take care not to damage any vulnerable parts of the keywork. When assembling the instrument, it is best to align first of all the wing and long joint adjacently, and insert them together into the butt grasping them both with the left hand. To disassemble, hold the butt firmly with the right hand, taking care not to place undue strain on any of the key-work, and remove the long joint first, grasping it with the left hand and carefully twisting it to disengage the tenon from the socket. When removing the wing, take care not to damage the linkage between butt and wing.

The 'Leak Factor'

Many players in the US are pre-occupied with the importance of maintaining the instrument 'bottle-tight' – that is, ensuring the there is a zero-rate 'leak factor' through either pads, joints or body. To achieve and maintain this is a time-consuming process, which can involve periodically immersing each joint in oil (having first removed all the keywork and posts) and sealing the pads with paraffin wax.

The ensuing benefits include:

- the resistance is lowered
- the sonority improved
- the attack of notes is made easier and safer
- downward slurring is facilitated
- lower levels of skill of breath / embouchure technique may be tolerated.

However the late Prof. Arthur Benade once pointed out that there is an acoustic penalty to pay. A modest leak factor will, by lowering and flattening the peaks of the resonance curves, offer pitch flexibility without loss of intensity; on the other hand a zero leak factor that renders them higher and steeper will cause a greater loss of resonance when any attempt is made to 'bend' the pitch of a note (Fig 1):

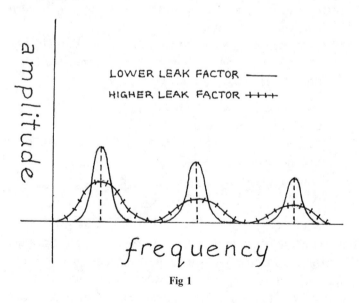

Fig 1

Four
In Performance

§4.1 Introduction

In the following sections the technique of playing is divided into constituent skills, identifying that part of the body responsible – from abdomen through to brain. Starting first with the fundamental question of Playing Position, in the section that follows wind-playing is examined in the context of a sporting activity. Each share common principles involving the use of mind over body to exercise fine control, utilizing our natural functions to support what is essentially an unnatural activity.

In those sections concerned with playing technique (§4.3 to §4.7 and §4.11 to §4.13) the material is organized under the following headings:

1   **Theory** - the underlying ideas applicable to the subject
2   **Application** – how these should be applied
3   **Routines** giving material to be practised, with brief explanations
4   **Faults / Problems**
5   **Other**

The concluding sections §4.8 to §4.10 and §4.14 to §4.18 deal with the other more practical aspects of performing.

With regard to the Practising Routines given below: some of these are comparatively demanding, being designed for those that are already more advanced and better equipped. Just as the regime prescribed at a purpose-built gymnasium for 'fitness training' would need to be designed to suit us each individually, here each player will need to select and modify these Routines to suit his own capabilities at any given time.

§4.2 Training: the 'Sport' of Wind-Playing

Parallels may be drawn between wind-playing and the practice of almost any sport*. These will prove illuminating for both student and teacher alike. All of the following principles should be found uncontroversial when related to sport; they are equally valid – adapting where necessary – for the playing of a wind instrument such as ours.

General

In any typical sport discipline, those performing at a con- spicuously high level will all tend to employ a characteristic style that is easily identifiable, while others whose style differs or deviates from this are unable to compete in terms of performance. We may thus confidently assert that the style of the former is 'good', is 'correct', while that of the others is 'poor', is 'wrong'. Thus in most sport disciplines there is a perceived 'style' which, in the opinion of experts, needs to be employed (more or less) in order to achieve optimum performance. Where a particular style is being employed that deviates from this, we may confidently predict that, after a certain point, further progress will be handicapped and curtailed.

However in order to achieve high performance, impec-

* The author acknowledges the article by Bengt Belfrage: (Belfrage, 1978) for some of the ideas expressed here.

cable style on its own is not enough. Technical skill needs to be combined with strength and stamina as well. It is therefore the coach's task to devise and implement training routines that

- inculcate the necessary skills
- provide a vehicle for style to be perfected and / or corrected
- build up the requisite stamina and strength.

It is self-evident that our level of performance, and even our capacity to absorb new skills, will closely depend on our general level of fitness: thus adequate diet, sleep and exercise are vital pre-requisites.

Equipment

At the outset of our training, our equipment needs to be checked. This comprises both the 'kit' we are wearing and the 'gear' we are using.

Regarding 'kit': are we dressed properly for the part? For most sports there is an accepted wardrobe that any serious participant will be expected to wear. Clothing should not restrict mobility or hamper performance in any way.

Regarding 'gear': is our equipment suitable for one of our experience, of our size, or of our strength? Equipment used by the expert may not always be suitable for the beginner; e.g. while the ski expert prefers skis that are long and stiff, the beginner will learn better using short and wide skis, only graduating to the others later. It needs to be serviceable, but without having to be up to the exacting standards required by the expert.

Training

To develop stamina and strength, the training session needs to challenge us to the limits of ability and endurance if maximum progress is to be achieved. Only the actual experiencing of this limit will help it to be surpassed.

A timepiece is a useful yardstick for identifying and documenting current ability and rate of progress.

When attempting to carry out any set task, the 'means whereby' we achieve it is more important than the end result. Instead of 'end gaining' for short term results, we should concentrate on employing techniques that are sound.

For a practice routine to be efficient, it needs to be simplistic enough for us to be able to monitor ourselves objectively whilst carrying it out.

In order for certain tasks to be carried out well, other skills must already have been mastered first. Thus the best training routine may be directed first at other things, and not necessarily be targetted towards the end-result.

We need to have mastered the basics first before starting to address more advanced demands. This calls for qualities of patience, humility, faith and realism.

To bring about the desired experience, the setting up of an artificial situation may often be necessary. This may be achieved by using either a training aid, or devising some routine that makes novel demands and poses unfamiliar challenges.

To master a new skill, we need not only to understand intellectually what we are trying to achieve, but to experience for ourselves the sensation of doing it.

When working on specific skills, even higher performance levels should be aimed for than those needed under normal circumstances.

The 'finished product' will require several different skills to be deployed all at once; having isolated them, we may then devise practice routines that target each of these specifically. They may then be exercised in various combinations.

When accidents have occurred during practice, or when faults have been detected, we need to take the time and trouble to determine what has caused them. Only when the root-cause has been correctly diagnosed can a remedy be prescribed and an effective treatment adopted. If a body-member has failed us, we may need to ask whether the fault was committed there, or the wrong order given?

Our best teacher will always remain ourselves. We should observe and appraise ourselves whilst in action.

New insights and experiences are gained through creative experimentation, and we need to set up special occasions to bring this about.

Preparing for Action

For the athlete to be able to perform at peak form, a process of 'warming-up' is necessary. An efficient warm-up routine needs to be delicately balanced between 'not enough' and 'too much'.

Performance nerves often occur when, awaiting our cue to start, we are plagued by distracting thoughts. These may be kept at bay if the brain is sufficiently involved in concentrating on the task in hand, thereby crowding out other distractions. Taking the maximum interest in all the multiple issues involved, while coming to understand them more and more, will help to furnish such food for thought.

In Action

Whilst 'performing', we rely mostly on automatic responses and reflexes. These will 'deliver' according to how they have been programmed. The skills available for deployment are those that have been furnished by our practice.

When the body is in action, it sends back many messages to the brain. While the beginner is insensitive to these and thus unaware of them, the expert has learned to apprehend them and is thus able to respond to them.

When in action, there are more important matters to be consciously aware of, and thus to monitor, than considerations of mere technique. We need to identify what these may be and to concentrate on them. These may relate to the avoidance of undue tension or how we are pacing ourselves.

Our activity calls for a considerable physical work, not to mention mental concentration. Such demands require us to husband our physical resources. Superfluous effort is not only wasteful but conflicting. If forces in one direction are counteracted by forces in the opposing direction, each will cancel the other out. Every unit of effort can be seriously diminished in its effect if it is hampered by tension *en route*. Thus the engaging of one set of muscles, while at the same time leaving other parts of the body uninvolved, is a necessary skill, and one that requires conscious effort to acquire. When skiers cross rough terrain the beginner, rigid throughout, works twice as hard as the expert who, with flexible ankles and knees, is thereby able to maintain poise in his upper body. While possible to run upstairs involving the entire body, one may choose to restrict effort to ankles and knees, thereby leaving the rest relatively uninvolved.

If an accident or mistake occurs during performance we should brazenly ignore it at the time rather than allow it to upset us; in this way we can maintain concentration and possibly prevent the recurrence of a later mishap.

The Bassoon

Conclusions

Applying these general principles to bassoon playing we may conclude:

- that certain mainstream guidelines must be adopted if maximum levels of performance are to be achieved
- we can assert with confidence that unless certain requirements are met, certain features of style employed, we will fail to achieve our maximum potential
- we can distinguish favourable patterns of use from those less so
- we can assert dogmatically that good style is achieved only by the application of correct principles.

§4.3   Playing Position

1   Theory

Playing position is here defined as the inter-relationship between player, body and instrument. The degree to which this is favourable or not will govern the efficiency of such crucial matters as breath-management and embouchure – and even finger technique. It is affected by such factors as:

- our own individual shape and size
- our posture when we play, standing or sitting; this can have an effect on our breathing (see §4.4)
- the method chosen to support the instrument; this will affect its location in relation to our arms and lips (see §3.2 *Accessories*)
- the angle of bend of the bocal; this affects the angle that we present the reed to our lips (see §4.5)

These need to be considered so that we can achieve an efficient and comfortable playing position.*

If the most important single component in bassoon-playing is breath and how we manage it (see §4.4), then the scope and efficiency of our breathing is largely dependent on 'good posture'. This might be defined as the condition intended by nature – the use primitive man made of his body, not adversely affected by such trappings of modern life as diet, clothes, being chair-bound etc. The better we use ourselves, the better the level of performance our bodies can deliver. Anything that interferes with our body-efficiency will handicap us as wind-players. The bassoon, being the shape, size and weight that it is, poses problems that each of us has to resolve individually. Much of our success as players depends on how we manage to cope with these problems.

There is a striking improvement in tone quality when an amateur choir at rehearsal, having sat down to sing, repeats a passage on its feet. Just as the orator would choose to deliver a public speech standing rather than sitting, it is arguable that standing to play offers advantages over being seated:

- the back muscles (which intertwine with those of the legs) have to be involved to a greater extent than when sitting, and these make an extra contribution to the support of the breath
- we can feel free to respond more directly and with less inhibition to the artistic demands of the moment
- changing the distribution of body weight on the legs can effect subtle changes to the support and control of breath.

* The author wishes to acknowledge the lessons in the Alexander Technique taken over the past 40 years and the valuable precepts that these have taught him.

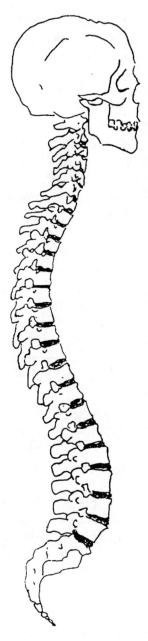

Fig 2

Thus for those occasions that call for maximum projection – such as playing a concerto or recital in public – the bassoonist will benefit from adopting a standing position. However as orchestral and ensemble players we are forced to spend the vast majority of our time playing seated. Since we need to consider the different implications involved, standing and sitting to play are dealt with separately below.

The balance achieved between the head, neck and spine is crucial for the efficient use of ourselves. If we look at an adult skeleton from the side, we will notice that there are three curves (see Fig 2). Starting from the pelvis, the backbone curves slightly forward; in the region of the shoulder blades it curves back again; the neck then comes forward, supporting the head. In some respects the spinal column may be compared with a pile of children's bricks: if instead of a straight column one is offset, then relative stability can only be achieved if the next one is placed so as to counterbalance it. For a balance to be achieved with minimum effort we need to hold the head – that relatively heavy member – in a position that is neither craned forward nor held back.

Our playing position should be one that presents the reed to the lips from straight in front (rather than at an oblique angle) and at an angle that is embouchure-friendly. Most players will need to customize their instrument and/ or accessories to suit their individual requirements (shape, size, jaw etc.) in order to help them achieve and maintain this (see §3.2 *Accessories*).

2 Application

Standing

Some early tutors forbade the student to practise except whilst standing; the reason was presumably that we are less

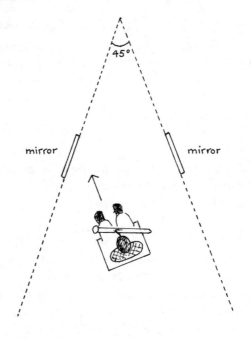

Fig 3

likely to adopt a faulty playing position when standing up than when sitting down. Whilst standing it is indeed possible to crane forward with the head or, at the other extreme, to hold the chin in and thrust the chest out; however the most comfortable way to stand is with the head, neck and back poised vertically in line so as best to counteract the effects of gravity and avoid undue stiffness. This may be compared with the stance adopted by the sentry, who needs to remain alert on guard-duty for an extended period. The shoulders are aligned with the hips and the feet are slightly apart (for the bassoonist, perhaps, with the left leading).

In this position our breathing apparatus has the maximum scope to operate freely. Ideally a way should be found to support the instrument in a location relative to the body so that the hands can reach the keys without strain, and so that the reed is presented to the lips at an 'embouchure-friendly' angle. See §3.2 *Accessories* for a discussion of available options.

To establish the most favourable position, we should ideally have a pair of mirrors – one ahead and one sited obliquely to the side at an angle of 45° – to enable us to check what we are doing in profile (see Fig 3). Stand up without the instrument and sense that everything looks and works well. We will be better able to observe what is actually happening to our back and hips if our clothes are not loose and baggy, since these will hide more then they show. We then bring the instrument into playing position without disturbing anything.

Sitting

Some teachers (notably in continental Europe), by only ever watching their students play standing, would appear to be uninterested in how they play when sitting. Nonetheless in the real world, practically all our playing in public will be done sitting. We face the problem that most chairs are not designed to serve as a satisfactory adjunct to playing. They are designed for rest and relaxation, rather than for working in – or to facilitate storage and transport. Their height cannot be adjusted, the seat is raked towards the back, or dished, or upholstered, their back sloped and thus unable to give support where needed. Some chairs have a straight rim at the side of the seat which interferes with the instrument. Each chair presents a different problem for us to solve if it is not to seduce us into sitting badly. It is often possible to cope with a problem chair as follows:

- raising the back legs with wooden blocks (or even one's shoes) to alter its angle
- stacking a second similar chair on top of the first to change its height and angle

65

- using a wedge-shaped cushion (see Fig 4b).
- perching on the front, or off-centre to one side – which means foregoing any back support
- if the seat is sloped or dished, turning the chair clockwise so that the back is on ones left side.

The important point is not to allow a poorly designed chair to prejudice an efficient playing position.

Each orchestral instrument poses different challenges for the player when seated. In certain orchestras the cellists have their own user-friendly model of chair; the bassoonist deserves similar consideration. In a given chair, the players of smaller woodwinds have more freedom of choice as to how they may choose to sit compared with us. Because of the design of the bassoon, which requires it to be held at the side of the body, and its weight, which needs an apparatus to support it, our choice is more restricted. As in standing, we must strive:

- to achieve an efficient playing position when seated
- to preserve the proper relationship of head, neck and spine, which is paramount
- to ensure that the breathing apparatus has maximum scope for operation.

The shoulders should remain in-line and unhunched and the chair height should permit heels to rest on the floor. In determining how we sit in the chair, we may also have to take into consideration the visibility of music stand and conductor.

An ideal set-up will allow the trunk to have freedom and scope for a little movement, uninhibited by the back of the chair. However, it is often beneficial if the back of the chair can offer some degree of support when required. While the pianist on his stool is forced to rely on his own back muscles to prevent collapse, the wind player, who has to deal with the different demands of lengthy rehearsal and

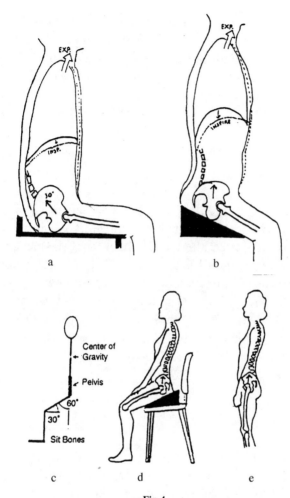

Fig 4
(We apologise for reproducing Fig 4 without the author's permission which we
made every effort to obtain)

performance duration, will usually require such support.

Dr Richard Norris in his *The Musician's Survival Manual* (Norris, 1993) has made a valuable contribution to this
debate, drawing attention to the effect that the sitting angle
has on the diaphragm: "Sitting with the hips and knees at
90 degrees tends to cause reversal of the lumbar curve, thus

67

The Bassoon

flattening the diaphragm and collapsing the chest, limiting full breathing (Fig 4a, b)". To combat this he advocates the use of a lightweight, portable wedge cushion to modify the existing chair seat: "the forward-sloping seat places the centre of gravity directly over the sitting bones (Fig 4c, d). This is similar to the standing position (Fig 4e)."

3 Routines

1   Stand and then sit to play in front of a mirror. Observe to what extent the angle of the instrument may have been altered. It is likely that the location of instrument relative to body will differ, according to whether we are standing or sitting to play; we should be aware of this fact and of its implications.
2   While seated in the chair, rock gently back and forth from a pivot at the base of the spine in order to experience the point of balance.

4 Faults / Problems

Certain problems of physical strain – from minor discomfort to major disabilities – may be attributable to having adopted a faulty playing position over a period of time. The most common fault is to allow the collapse of the bottom of the spine against the back of the chair.

Other faults to avoid include:

● twisting of the upper body, caused by holding the left shoulder forward, the right shoulder back
● hunching the shoulders
● holding the right elbow too far back
● arching the right wrist

- taking the reed between the lips at an angle other than that of a right-angle from each side
- crossing the legs
- extending the feet forwards
- gripping with the legs under the chair.

Some problems encountered can be due to the very considerable weight of the modern instrument. The adopting of a more user-friendly playing position might require the altering of such accessories as crook or support-system (see §3.2).

§4.4   Abdomen / Breath-Leading

1   Theory

After playing position, matters concerning breath and how we use it need to be considered next. This, to the wind player, is what bowing is to the string player. Such basic elements as tone production, control of nuance, phrasing (especially in slow tempi), tone quality, intonation, projection all depend on the quality of our breath and how we use it. The term that best describes the techniques of directing and managing our breath is the German word *Atemführung*, here translated as 'breath-leading'.

   While nature endows each of us with the basic resources for achieving these results, we can all achieve some measure of improvement through training. Although breathing is a continuous and largely unconscious process its harnessing for playing purposes requires awareness of the mechanics involved. Our aim must be:

- to develop the control we exert over our breath, enhancing the awareness and obedience of abdominal muscles, and promoting their independence and strength

69

The Bassoon

- to maximise the supply of wind available to us in playing
- to achieve localized work, unaccompanied by conflicting tensions or negative participation elsewhere in the body.

A basic problem in the teaching of breath-leading, and in the raising of our awareness of how we breathe, is that most of the processes involved are concealed, being invisible both to us and to a teacher. While problems of tone-production on a stringed instrument can be easily diagnosed, most aspects of bowing technique being outwardly visible, the wind player cannot rely to the same extent on external observation and thus has to develop other means of perception.

As in other athletic pursuits, the scope for improvement and development should motivate and encourage us. Practice will in time improve the quality, and enlarge the capacity, of breath at our disposal. Like the athlete who measures his progress with the aid of a stop-watch, we should use timed practice routines to evaluate our current level of ability and chart our future progress.

Before considering the technique of breath-leading from the point of view of bassoon playing, let us consider first some of the different breathing options available. The lung capacity of the average adult (ca 4.5 litres – all amounts given here are approximations) may be divided into four components (Fig 5):

- Tidal Air: the volume of air (ca 0.5 litres) respired involuntarily when at rest
- Supplemental Air: the volume of air (ca 1.5 litres) that it is possible to expire with conscious effort at the end of the preceding
- Residual Air: the volume of air (ca 1 litre) that remains in the lungs after all conscious effort to expire. Residual Air cannot be expired.

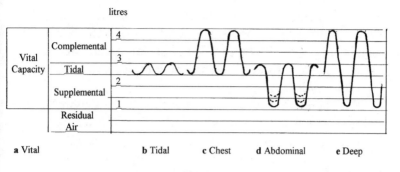

Fig 5

- Complemental Air: the volume of air (ca1.5 litres) that it is possible to inspire with conscious effort over and above Tidal Air, to fill the lungs to their maximum.

The total volume of respirable air (Complemental Air + Tidal Air + Supplemental Air) is termed Vital Capacity (ca3.5 litres) (Fig 5a).

During Tidal Breathing (Fig 5b), inspiration is produced by the downward push of the contracting diaphragm and the expansion of the chest caused by the slight spreading and lifting of the ribs by the intercostal muscles. Expiration is produced by the elastic recoil of the lungs, ribs and other abdominal components. To breathe in Complemental Air, we employ Chest Breathing (Fig 5c), during which the upper chest is filled by expanding and raising the rib-cage while at the same time the diaphragm strongly contracts. To breathe out the Complemental Air comparatively little effort is necessary as the chest will deflate, once we allow it to, through its own natural elasticity and weight.

To breathe out the Supplemental Air, we use Abdominal Breathing (Fig 5d), during which we contract the muscles of the abdominal wall, causing the abdominal contents to push the diaphragm upwards and diminish the capacity of the chest. To breathe in the Supplemental Air, again little or no effort is necessary. The reason is that, as soon as we cease to apply pressure, the natural recoil of the body will cause air to be drawn in effortlessly. In Deep Breathing, (Fig 5e), these three patterns are combined to produce a maximum degree of respiration.

Playing a wind instrument requires that over long periods of time a steady stream of air be sent through the lips under a controlled pressure. The pattern of exhalation best answering these demands is Abdominal Breathing, formerly called 'diaphragm breathing' by those supposing the necessary support to be generated there, but a misconception since physiologists now consider the diaphragm to be exclusively a muscle of inspiration.

The advantages of Abdominal Breathing are many:

- the muscles employed have almost unlimited strength and stamina. To withstand a heavy blow to the torso it is these that we would brace, contriving to have less, rather than more, air in our body.
- in addition to being very strong, these muscles can be trained to exercise control over the breath being sent into the instrument in subtle ways. These include maintaining the air at an even pressure, and modulating it by applying nuance for *crescendo* / *diminuendo* effects, accents and vibrato.
- instead of being deliberate and effortful, as in chest breathing, the inspiration is not only rapid but both automatic and effortless. The intake of new breath will be greatly favoured the more we can sustain the breath pressure so that as much as possible of the Supplemental Air is exhausted (see dotted lines in Fig 5d). Here we may consider the analogy of the coiled bedspring (Fig 6). If a spring (Fig 6a) is compressed (b), it will on release return to its original shape with a certain degree of recoil. But if it is compressed even more (Fig 6c), the degree of recoil on release will be correspondingly greater.

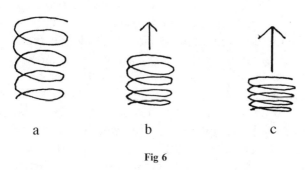

a   b   c

Fig 6

With practice we should be able to extend the trough of the inverse peak (Fig 5d) so that the amount of Supplemental and Tidal Air taken in is adequate to service all our normal playing requirements. Chest breathing need only be used to add Complemental Air to Tidal and Supplemental Air for the execution of exceptional tasks – such as sustained phrases requiring an unusual amount of wind or abnormally long held notes (Fig 5e). In time we will achieve enhanced awareness in these abdominal muscles, so that whilst playing we will feel the cockpit of direction to be based here, from where we match the varied demands of tessitura, dynamics and vibrato with suitable support of the air column.

2   Application

Avoiding the traditional practice adopted by many – which is to commence to play by first taking in a breath, and raising the upper body to do so – we should rather prepare to breathe by first of all exhaling, and then letting go. In this way we may experience the reflex sensation of effortless resumption to the peak point of Tidal Volume. By neglecting to inhale consciously before starting to play, the rib-cage will remain somewhat less involved in the breathing process. The rib-cage should not be allowed to

73

sink or collapse whilst the abdominal muscles are working; the playing position adopted should enable our skeleton to maintain a stable scaffolding, within the framework of which our breathing apparatus can freely operate. During this process of controlled exhalation we should commence by activating the muscles at the very base of the abdomen just above the groin; these we normally involve in such actions as carefully coughing up a bone lodged in the throat, or when we attempt to excrete. As exhalation proceeds, the point of control will appear to rise up towards the base of the ribs. We may compare with to the squeezing of toothpaste out of a tube by starting from the very bottom (Fig 7). If we were to squeeze higher up near the centre, the contents would be forced downwards as well as upwards. In blowing the bassoon, we are supporting a column of air that we may imagine as starting from the bottom of the pelvis and extending unimpeded straight up the windpipe into the instrument – similar to a fountain jet where a steady pressure from below maintains erect and stable a vertical column of water.

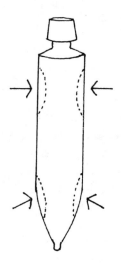

Fig 7

Our study must be to develop the awareness, control and obedience of our abdominal muscles and to promote their independence and strength. We must restrict our effort to this so that we may avoid as far as possible unhelpful sympathetic involvement elsewhere – such as in the upper part of the body – which would cause conflicting and unproductive tensions and even cancel out the net result. How much pressure we apply will vary according to the demands of the musical phrase – whether it is high or low, loud or soft etc. We can detect these variations in pressure by placing a finger on the flanks whilst playing. The finger will be pushed out according to the varying tension in the musculature of the abdominal wall. Towards the end of the breath this effort has to be increased in order to prevent the effect of a *diminuendo*.

When preparing to play, instead of a deliberate in-breath to 'top-up' in readiness, we should breathe out some supplemental air and use the subsequent relaxed in-flow of breath as a preparatory 'up-beat'. In this way we will secure a good attack and avoid having more wind on board than we need. It should normally be possible to use up all our breath playing without having to exhale stale air before taking in fresh (in the case of the oboe this does not apply, because of its comparatively small air consumption).

It is a good idea, and often revealing, to have an independent check on what is actually happening; we can do this in two ways:

- by practising unclothed in front of a mirror we can use sight to verify and supplement what we are being told by our bodily sensations and feelings
- by touching relevant parts of the body with a free hand whilst we play, we can identify the muscles we wish to employ and effectively communicate with them.

Such exercises as sustaining long tones, by their minimum

demands on our concentration, can liberate the mind and thus:

- offer us a rare opportunity to observe objectively and critically assess ourselves in action
- try out creative experiments, offer ourselves novel experiences

The muscles employed in breath-leading will be trained and strengthened if we also take part in sporting activities such as swimming and walking.

3 Routines

Note that these are primarily to heighten awareness and control; see §4.7 and §4.12 for further routines to develop stamina and strength.

Without Instrument

1 Learn awareness and independent control of the abdominal muscles avoiding involvement elsewhere – especially of the rib-cage and shoulders
   - practice deep abdominal breathing lying on the floor with the head on a book, knees up, backbone flat, shoulder-blades in contact with the floor (Fig 8a)

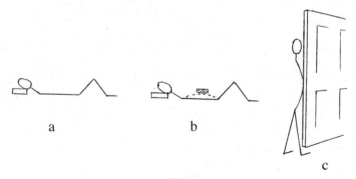

a   b

                                                        c

Fig 8

- now balance a pile of heavy books on the lower abdomen and, with your breathing, make them rise and fall (Fig 8b).

2   experience the abdominal muscles at work by standing with feet slightly apart in front of an open door so as to lean the abdomen slightly against it; the tensing of the abdominal wall will push us away from the door (Fig 8c).

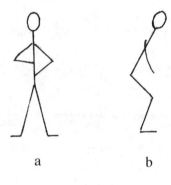

a   b

Fig 9

3   'Dog-pants': to exercise our abdominal muscles independently we imitate the rapid panting of a dog:
- standing up, with one hand on the chest and the other placed lightly on the abdomen, make rapid shallow breaths in and out, whilst avoiding any involvement of the rib-cage in movement. With our hands we can thus distinguish those parts that are moving from those that remain uninvolved (Fig 9a)
- in order to involve and activate the back muscles adopt a 'skiing' position – knees and hips bent, head and spine lined up – maintaining a hand each on chest and abdomen (Fig 9b).

   Varying speeds will be used to carry out both this exercise and others later on. In order to avoid having constantly to alter metronome settings, the following system dispenses with having to use a metronome. The second being a familiar interval of time-measurement and thus easy to calculate mentally, we adopt two seconds (or ♩ = 30) as our universal beat against which we sub-divide differing numbers of units. Our 'dog-panting' in-out will now be gentle, but at a precisely controlled tempo of successively six, seven, eight and nine per beat. The group of seven (septuplet) may be subdivided either 4 + 3 or 3 + 4, while nine may best be thought of first as a slow triplet, with each beat then subdivided into triplets 3 + 3 + 3 (Fig 10):

Fig 10

- repeat the group of six as above, but now increase the amount of air breathed in and out until the maximum is reached; take care to stop before hyper-ventilation causes dizziness (!).

4   Check and promote the steady control of breath by proceeding to blow through the reed in order to produce a sustained crow – like a husky croak. To produce this particular sound – known in the U.S. as 'triple-crow' because it combines high, middle and low frequencies – a favourable balance of support between the muscles of the abdomen and those of the embouchure has to be achieved (it is also necessary for the reed itself to possess a reasonably favourable degree of adjustment). The lips need to be loose, the jaw comparatively open, but the wind support not inconsiderable, otherwise the reed will refuse to respond. If the embouchure is too tight or if too much reed is taken

into the mouth the reed will produce merely a high-pitched crow.

- sustain a stable signal*, while you sense the precise degree of abdominal support required; note how the signal will respond like a barometer to the smallest fluctuation of support.

- produce a cycle of three sustained crows, each of maximum duration, with timed in-breaths (Fig 11); count off the beats @ ♩ = 60 in units of five – utilizing this indivisible time-unit of five (which corresponds to the number of our fingers) will be found superior to one of three or four. Aim to achieve a progressive improvement in score over the course of practice.

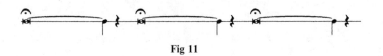

Fig 11

5   practise the control of rate of air-flow, the ability to maintain an even stream of breath:

- blow at a lighted candle held one foot away from the lips so as to cause the flame to 'lie down' horizontally and remain as still as possible (Fig 12).

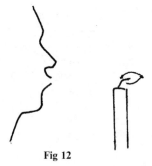

Fig 12

* signal in the acoustical sense to mean the emitted sound.

The Bassoon

- practise with the so-called 'Incentive Spirometer' (Fig 13), as advocated by Arnold Jacobs (1915-1998), the famous US teacher and tuba player. This device is used in hospitals to give respiratory patients a visual demonstration of how much air they can inhale; blowing through a tube, one has to maintain a white ball vertically stable.

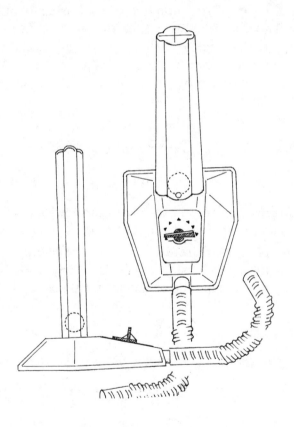

Fig 13

With Instrument

6 Long notes: the practice of long sustained tones is a classic training routine that cannot be bettered for the development of stamina and control, and as a mechanism for self-appraisal and experiment.

- cycle of repeated low C♯s, *poco forte, senza diminuendo, senza vibrato*, with timed in-breaths, each sustained for as many beats as possible (to a count in units of five as in Fig 11 above). Sounding this particular note promotes good style, being one that, by its demand of air, will encourage an open jaw (Fig 14):

poco forte senza dim.

Fig 14

- *Sons filés** for checking evenness of tone and matching of intonation; sequences of notes in *poco forte, senza vibrato*, moving away from the centre of the range (d in alternation with d♯) in whole-tone steps. This routine should be adapted so as to fully exploit available breath capacity: thus according to individual stamina arrange so that each sequence is longer or shorter, each tone sustained for either four or three beats (Fig 15):

Fig 15

* *sons filés*: French term for a series of repeated tones.

7   Dynamics: we need to maximise our range of available dynamic, with the aim of matching that of clarinet and horn.

  • the developing of *crescendo* and loud playing skills: increase intensity by terraced increments (since this makes it easier to pace growth); range of a seventh down and up from d / e♭; sequence of nine (or six) tied quavers (Fig 16):

Fig 16

  • the developing of soft playing skills, striving for minimum intensity through minimum effort. Practise first re-iterated accents in free time on a mid-register note; after initial attack diminish instantly, aiming to reach ever more rapidly the point of minimum expenditure of effort; verify that the subtle breath nuances result in clearly audible accents (Fig 17):

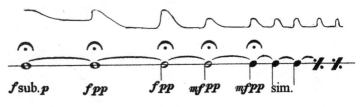

Fig 17

  • practise these next in time at semitone intervals over the same range (Fig 18)
  • developing *diminuendo* skills, a pattern of control which in theory should mirror that of *crescendo* in

Fig 18

reverse: after shorter *crescendo* to maximum loudness, decrease intensity by terraced increments as above; achieve by a relaxing and lessening of effort ('give less to get less') whilst, rather than by tensing and constricting, withdrawing the reed from the lips as necessary (Fig 19):

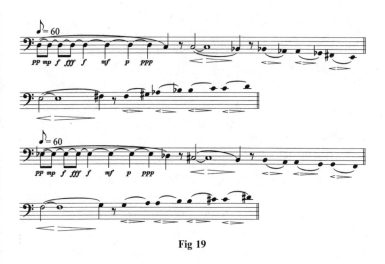

Fig 19

8   Experience relying exclusively on abdominal support by foregoing any assistance from the embouchure; try to sound the instrument having taken the entire reed as far as (and beyond) the 'Turk's head' wrapping in the mouth; the precise amount of effort required will depend in part on the individual reed's threshhold of resistance:

Fig 20

- try first the lower register chromatically from d (Fig 20a, next page):
- ascending from d, notice how the pitch of e requires extra support to raise it into tune (Fig 20b)
- ascending beyond e, notice a similar phenomenon with regard to c′ (Fig 20c).

9 use breath support alone, without aid of the tongue, to articulate (see §4.6 Routine 8, p121).

4 *Faults / Problems*

- commencing to play by first taking in a breath, and raising the upper body to do so
- allowing the rib-cage to sink or collapse whilst the abdominal muscles are working
- excessive use of 'chest-breathing' (see above)
- giving insufficient support to the column of air, thereby requiring excess embouchure support to compensate
- hampering the activity of the abdominal muscles by wearing anything too tight around the waist, such as tight belts and jeans; these will de-sensitize our awareness and also encourage undue compensatory chest involvement
- Touching our abdomen while we play can lead to some confusion. If we place the flat of the hand lightly whilst blowing out, we will feel it being drawn in as this part of the body shrinks. On the other hand, if we poke two fingers in the same place, we feel them being pushed out. The explanation is that it is the muscle tone of the

abdominal wall which becomes progressively under greater tension, thereby causing the fingers to be pushed out. Similarly if we feel with finger and thumb the muscles of the fore-arm when relaxed, as we tense them their expansion will push our fingers out.

5 *Other*

Circular (or Rotary) Breathing. This is the name given to a technique of breathing of great antiquity – also used by glass blowers and players of certain folk instruments – where the player avoids interrupting the flow of notes by breathing in through the nose while he is using his cheeks to expel the air. This technique is eminently possible on the bassoon; the resistance of the vibrating reed allows for a stable reservoir of air in the mouth to be maintained sufficiently to sustain the sound whilst inhaling. It can be usefully employed on occasions when a long note or phrase would otherwise be spoilt by a stop for breath (though its excessive use in solo work is to be deprecated on artistic grounds). The following preliminary exercises should be mastered first:

- using the back of the tongue to seal off the throat above the soft palate, open the jaw and fill the cheeks with air; then use the fingers of each hand to squeeze the air out through the mouth
- having filled the mouth with water, squirt it through pursed lips in a jet for as far a distance as possible
- having filled the cheeks with air, use them to blow a long controlled 'raspberry', at the same time breathing through the nose
- blow through a straw into a bowl of water, maintaining a steady flow of bubbles
- repeat these exercises whilst now breathing through the nose at the same time.

The Bassoon

When trying on the instrument, it is best to start with a friendly high-register note such as tenor g♯′ that speaks easily and is tolerant of disturbances to the rate of air-flow. The main problems concern:

- inflating cheeks and lowering jaw to form air reservoir without disturbing our playing
- having enough 'mouth air' for the duration required to breathe
- the effect on the embouchure while the cheeks are being squeezed
- achieving a smooth transition from 'mouth air' to 'abdominal air'.

In different registers and at different dynamics the pressure required will be found to vary.

§4.5   Mouth / Embouchure

1.   Theory

We have already considered the important role of the abdomen in regulating the quality of air needed by the instrument; the action of lip and reed will affect it no less. The placement and use of our lips when we play is commonly called the 'embouchure'. Its principal role is to complement the abdominal musculature in delivering, via the reed, wind of the quality and quantity needed to drive the instrument. It is also employed for a number of other important tasks. In addition to helping the note to speak punctually, these include the subtle modification of intonation, dynamic and colour (when required). When starting to play on a cold instrument, it is on the embouchure that we largely rely to help us get into tune. Generally speaking however, its role is subordinate to that of the breath; over-dependence on the embouchure may be considered as being symptomatic of insufficient breath-leading skills.

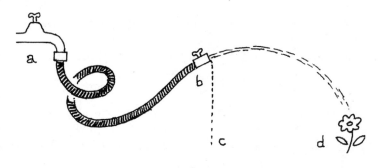

Fig 21

The way that the abdominal musculature and embouchure work in harness together may be illustrated by the image of using a garden hose (Fig 21). To water the flowers at **d**, we must regulate both the pressure of water admitted through the tap at **a** and the aperture of the nozzle at **b**. If the pressure at **a** is high, the spray of water can reach **d** with the nozzle **b** comparatively open. But if we reduce the pressure at **a**, the water will only arrive as far as **c**; to reach **d** we would need to introduce a greater degree of resistance to the flow of water by reducing the nozzle aperture at **b**. By analogy our embouchure and reed acts like a valve regulating the supply of air into the instrument. For the instrument to emit a signal at a desired pitch and degree of intensity, the air column inside the instrument needs to be excited by a sufficient pressure and quantity of air. If we can furnish enough of this pressure, then the contribution required of our embouchure (i.e. the supporting pressure applied to the reed by the lip muscles) need be only comparatively modest – assuming the use of a free-blowing reed. But the less we support our breath from below, the lower its pressure will be, and the more the musculature of the mouth will have to compensate for the deficiency by stepping up its pressure on the reed. Now if we compare

The Bassoon

the strength and stamina of the abdominal muscles to that of the lips, it is self-evident that we should try to take as much of the strain as possible from down below. Failure to do this (together with the habitual use of stiff reeds) will tempt the player to overrate the importance of his embouchure. We should think of it as a moderator rather than a prime element of control – a washer providing an air-tight seal between mouth and instrument.

Air driven through the reed causes it to vibrate. Our use of the embouchure, by a subtle contact with the vibrating blades, brings these diverse patterns of vibration under the player's control; ideally it should influence them positively, rather than inhibit them negatively. Although unaware of all the subtleties involved, when playing we can sense when support, embouchure and reed are happily collaborating by the enhanced strength of the resulting signal.

Together with breath-leading, embouchure skills are particularly relied on for the following tasks:

- Accuracy in pitching. While, thanks to its increased number of tone-holes, the pitching of notes is more foolproof on the modern than the period bassoon, the accurate deployment of fingers is hardly sufficient on its own to achieve this – the most common cause of wrong notes (especially in slurred passages) will not lie in the fingering. On our instrument there are many fingerings that can be made to produce more than one single pitch, according to the setting of embouchure and breath-leading adopted (see Fig 27 p104). If the setting we adopt is too wide of the mark, the wrong harmonic – in the form of an unwanted pitch or multiphonic – will sound instead.
- Timing. The timing of our entry depends no less on the same factors; a note cannot be relied on to speak punctually unless these settings, well-judged and in balance, are in place.

- Attack. The attack, or initiation of the note's speech, similarly calls for nice judgment if it is to be free of unwanted accent. Unless we are making a deliberate *sforzando* it should start without a bump. The sound also needs to commence without any undesirable element of noise, such as the 'cracking' effect caused when we neglect to use the 'flick technique' (see §4.8).

Other occasions when the embouchure may be required to exercise sensitive control include:

- the 'humouring' of problematic notes by helping them to match by ironing out discrepancies of pitch and response
- helping the security of 'fake' fingerings and 'fake' trills (see §4.8) and improving their quality.

Embouchure efficiency will govern our capacity to exercise this sensitive control. Factors we should consider affecting embouchure efficiency are:

1 the pressure applied to the reed by the lip musculature
2 the support to the lips afforded by the teeth behind, determined by the degree to which the jaws are open
3 how much reed we take into the mouth – i.e. whereabouts on the reed lip pressure is applied
4 the spot on each reed-blade that we target for the application of lip control.

1 To form an embouchure we curl back the lips – or rather the fleshy rear part of each lip – over the front teeth sufficiently to form a cushion between them and the reed (this is known to clarinettists as a 'double-lip embouchure') (Fig 22, next page). If the player's lips are thicker, he will need to distort his face less than if they are thin. The lips close around the reed to form an airtight seal. To help us do this we are endowed with a

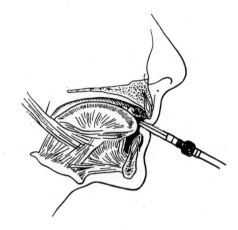

Fig 22

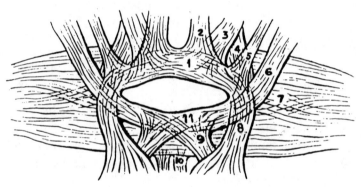

Fig 23
1, orbicularis oris (upper lip portion). 2, levator labii sup., alæque nasi. 3, levator labii superioris. 4, levator anguli oris. 5, zygomaticus minor. 6, zygomaticus major. 7, buccinator. 8, depressor anguli oris. 9, depressor labii inferioris. 10, mentalis. 11, orbicularis oris (lower lip portion).

remarkable apparatus of muscles that resemble the radiating spokes of a bicycle wheel. Fig 23 shows the various muscles and identifies them by name. Of these, it is the circumferential lip-muscle (*orbicularis oris*) that plays the most important role, which is similar to that of the drawstring of a purse when tightened; however we should try to equalize out the effort between this and the other muscles, as we do when we whistle or kiss. If we insert a finger into the mouth of a breast-fed baby (who has to place unique reliance on this muscular apparatus), we can feel this all-round lip effort being exercised. While these muscles possess relatively little strength and stamina, they are nonetheless responsive to training.

2   The pressure applied to the reed by the lip muscles will be notably assisted by that of the teeth behind. Indeed to close our jaws is such a natural reflex that we are hardly aware when we do so, or of expending any effort in the process. However we should ideally keep our jaws as open as possible when we play; this is in order to maximize the oral cavity to lend resonance to the tone, and to help free the throat and keep it open. We should not 'bite' the reed through the lips, as if holding it in a carpenter's vice clamping from above and below; this could allow air to escape from the sides of the mouth, leading to disturbing noise and loss of control. All of this means relying as much as possible on our lip muscles. With adequate breath support, the demands should be modest enough for them to be able to manage without having to rely on undue assistance from the teeth. Of course, much depends on having a reed with a comparatively low threshhold of resistance – one that requires minimum effort to make it speak. The dynamic chosen will usually affect the degree to which the jaw is open; e.g. very loud requires a wider jaw-opening to accommodate the increased wind, *crescendo* requires a progressive opening of the jaw.

3   How much of the reed we take into the mouth – i.e. whereabouts on the reed we exercise control with our lips – affects both the effort demanded and the results achieved:

More reed in the mouth, while favouring the speech of the upper register, will require a tighter grip to control the reed aperture, because of the increased arching and contouring higher up the blades. It can also have the following effects:

- sharpness of pitch overall
- poor attack of bass notes
- impaired control of pitch and stability.

Less reed in the mouth, while favouring the speech of the low register, will demand less lip-pressure to control the reed aperture. It can also have the following effects:

- flatness of pitch overall
- impaired tone quality.

For every register of the instrument there is an optimum point on each blade where the lip-pressure applied will favour the patterns of vibration. The interaction of lip and blade is subtle, acting both to dampen and select vibrations. Just as the bass-player must gauge the optimum point of contact on the string and his bow pressure, the bassoonist must select his correct point of contact on the blades and the pressure applied (Fig 24):

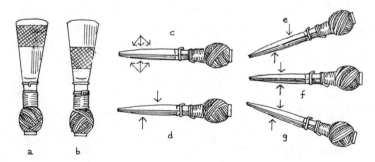

Fig 24

If the point of contact adopted is too wide of this ideal spot, loss of responsiveness and dampening of tone quality may result. For the best results this point should be located between the tip and centre of each blade **(a)** rather than between the centre and the collar **(b)**. In order to suit different registers and articulations, as well as to modify the intonation and tone colour, we can momentarily alter this control point in either direction by slightly moving the instrument in or out. It is possible to do this whilst essentially leaving the lips in place, without shifting the lip-flesh along the reed-blade **(c)**.

4 The spot on each reed-blade that we target for the application of lip control – indeed the whole question of 'reed-angle in mouth' – is a matter usually not considered by players and determined entirely by chance. If we accept that for each register there is a specific area of reed that is best for optimum control and response, then it follows that this ideal point for lip-contact must be the same for each blade. Thus an embouchure where the pressure points are located correspondingly on each blade **(c)** is more efficient than one where they are not **(d)**. This is because, in the latter case, much of the upper blade towards the tip is uncontrolled by the lip – vibrating 'wild' – while the lower blade risks being over-damped. There is also reduced scope for modifying the amount of reed in the mouth; even less of the upper blade is controlled when further in, while further out the lower lip is too close to the tip.

To ensure that our lip contact-points correspond on each reed-blade, three factors need to be considered:

a the individual shape of our jaw
b the angle at which we present the reed to our embouchure
c the bend of our crook.

a The jaw formation of every player is different; most of us diverge in some way from the 'chimpanzee bite', where upper and lower sets of teeth meet and close perfectly together. With such a bite, the reed may enter at right angles (Fig 24f). For most of us a slightly protruding upper jaw ('overbite') is more common than a slightly protruding lower jaw ('prognathous bite'). With a greater or lesser degree of 'overbite', such a horizontal angle of entry would result in the upper lip being closer to the wires of the reed than the lower (Fig 24d).

b The angle at which the reed is taken in the lips greatly affects the efficiency of the embouchure. In the case of the oboe, the player will, without thinking, place the reed in the position where his lips would like it to be; the size and shape of his instrument gives him the freedom to do this by tilting either head or instrument. By comparison the bassoonist is forced to operate within a strait-jacket. When playing, this angle of reed to embouchure is governed by these factors:

- size and shape of the player – relative length of neck, arms etc
- location of instrument in relation to the player's body, determined by the method of instrument support adopted, and often varying as to whether hc or she is sitting or standing
- the individual bend of crook (see below).

Although those tutors that deal with, and illustrate, this specific topic (e.g. Seltmann & Angerhöfer, Terëkhin) are doctrinaire in the angle they prescribe, they notably fail to agree with each other (!). A glance at several bassoonists together will usually reveal a considerable divergence of reed angle (see Pl 11).

c The bend of our crook. This has varied much in historical times, the shape being designed to favour

Plate 11
Reed-angle: diversity demonstrated by Karl Oehlberger and Rudolf Hanzl,
Vienna Philharmonic Orchestra, London 1948.

archaic embouchure practices no longer in use today*. It is hardly standardized even today. The experience of horn-players – who prefer their leading mouth-pipe to be longer straight, rather than bending sooner – indicates that an acute-angled bend near the tip of the crook (quite apart from its capacity for collecting water) might prejudice air-wave transmission. In any case, its shape should be determined according to requirement.

The lip contact-points on each blade will correspond least when the player with an overbite is presented with his reed entering downwards into his mouth (Fig 24e, Pls 12, 13). Here not only can he exert little control over the upper blade, but he has minimum scope for shifting his reed further in or out. He can however solve the problem by arranging a downwards reed-angle (Fig 24g).

'Reed-in-mouth' considerations will determine the location of the reed-tip inside the mouth, which can affect the working of the tongue (see §4.6).

Having considered the role played by the lip muscles and the jaw, there remains that of the throat to consider. It should be maintained free and open in order to maximize the oral cavity, otherwise the resultant constriction might prejudice the quality of the sound (i.e. the spectrum of overtones present).

---

* It is axiomatic that the embouchure recommended here is designed for a modern bassoon technique employing modern-type reeds on the German-system instrument. Pictorial sources from earlier centuries show that crooks were often bent in such a way as to introduce the reed at a steep angle from above; crooks of this shape survive today, together with the original cases with the moulded housings that accepted them. It was also customary (especially in France) for the player to position the reed between his lips at an oblique angle. A mechanical advantage accrued from these procedures when long and heavy reeds were in use.

Plate 12
Reed angle: adverse effects of poor playing position (reproduced from Hubert
Clifford, *The School Orchestra*, London 1939 p 68).

The Bassoon

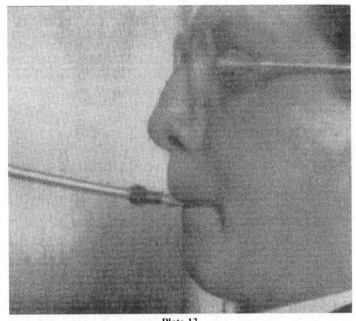

Plate 13
Reed-angle: common combination of down-slanting crook with overbite
(professional Berlin bassoonist, reproduced from Kurt Schlenger, *Beiträge zur
Physiologie und Pädagogik des Blasinstrumentenspiels*, Dresden 1935 p 30).

2   *Application*

To form the embouchure, we should begin relaxed, and
then only involve those muscles we need. With a 'user-
friendly' reed, it should not be necessary to form the lips
(as it were) into a scabbard to sheathe an imaginary sword.
Instead we should try closing our eyes and imagining we
are bringing a filled glass to our lips. On its approach,
notice the jaw relaxing and throat opening. Now we may
try this same procedure with the reed. As we bring it into
our mouth, we encircle it with the lips, but maintaining the
jaw relaxed. Holding the reed, we should try to produce a
solid, gutteral crow, applying no more than the amount of
lip pressure demanded by its degree of resistance. Observe

not only the relationship between the support of embouchure and that of wind, but also the extent to which pressure by the lips affects the crow.

The best way to verify our own optimum angle of reed-entry is to place the reed between the lips; as we form our embouchure and sound it, we allow it to adopt its natural angle relative to our lips and bite. Use a pair of mirrors (see Fig 3, p64) to observe in profile what this is. The crook we use should ideally be of such a shape that, when in playing position, the reed is presented to the lips at this correct angle, and that this angle of reed-entry can be maintained during playing. To achieve this, it might be found necessary to alter the angle of bend in our crook (see §7.3).

It is vital to achieve independence of function in different parts of the body – to keep those muscles loose and free that are not needed for a particular activity. This requires care and attention; cf the skier crossing rough terrain (§4.2 *In Action*). For much of our waking hours we unconsciously activate the muscles of our lower jaw to prevent it from sagging. However, it is possible for us to learn how to control these muscles by keeping them loose – this is, after all, what we have to do in order to gargle or swallow. Similarly in playing, it is important to keep the jaw free and the throat open in order to improve tone quality (as we have seen above).

For the note to 'speak' with the least effort, lip contact needs to be at that spot on the reed in general, and on each reed blade in particular, that collaborates best with its mode of vibration. A good way to identify this spot is to try to start the note without the aid of the tongue. This exercise will help us to discover by trial and error what the optimum settings are for a particular note: it will demonstrate how almost every each note calls for its own particular 'recipe', or combination of these two factors. Some notes (especially in the lower register) will demand a greater accuracy of setting, while others have varying degrees of tolerance. If and when this embouchure setting has been well chosen, the note will speak punctually. On trying this over the whole range of the instrument we will notice how we need to alter the siting of the lips on the reed according to the register – low register closer to the tip, high register closer to the wires. It is important to develop our awareness of the amount of reed in the mouth – i.e. where in each register the ideal nodal point is situated; we can feel with our tongue how far behind the lips and teeth the tip is located. When ascending from low to high register, we find the reed progressively drawn in automatically; however when descending, the reverse process of withdrawing the reed has to be conscious and deliberate.

Just as we can sharpen the pitch of a note by progressively tightening the embouchure, it is also possible to flatten its pitch by doing the opposite. To do this requires

- the use of a flexible, balanced reed with a sufficient tip aperture width
- control with the lips at the extreme tip of the reed
- extreme looseness of embouchure
- increased wind pressure, delivered by enhanced abdominal support.

3 Routines

Without Instrument

1 First practise keeping the jaw loose and free, isolating muscles needed for a particular activity from those that are not needed:
    - taking hold of our chin between finger and thumb, release the lower jaw so that we can move it up and down
    - set a greater challenge in maintaining the jaw muscles free by allowing someone else to do this.

2 An isometric* exercise to develop awareness and strength in all of the various lip muscles:

- dangle a heavy pen from the lips, rotating the head so as to make it describe a circle.
- Now carefully repeat this exercise using reed attached to crook. When the crook swings in a 360° circle, the reed will have to be gripped by all of the lip muscles in turn. Take care not to allow it to fall out of the mouth once the muscles begin to tire.

3 Exercises with the reed on its own, to demonstrate the role played by our lips and heighten our awareness of the lip muscles:

- crow it, trying to produce as wide a range as possible, from the deepest gutteral crow up to the highest screech
- try to produce sustained tones, rather than unmusical squawks; although the range available will depend on individual reed quality, it should be possible to achieve notes within the interval of an octave
- isolate these different muscle settings by improvising a little tune.

4 Practise now with the reed on the crook, to experience somewhat greater resistance. If we adopt the settings required for a normal mid-register note, depending on circumstances the resulting note should sound c♯′ or d′.

- practise raising the pitch in each of the following differing ways:
  - by tightening the lip muscles
  - by progressively closing the jaw, thereby increasing the pressure applied through the lips by the teeth

---

* isometric = equalizing in measure.

101

The Bassoon

-    by giving more support to the wind supply through the abdominal muscles.
- now try, by opening the jaws, to flatten this initial note by a semitone.
- for this exercise in tuneful crowing, employ only the muscles of the lips (Fig 25):

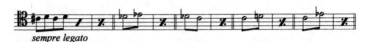

sempre legato

Fig 25

- produce and sustain a high pitch until the lip muscles start to collapse through fatigue.

With Instrument

5   Create a situation that makes enhanced demands on our breath and embouchure skills by wedging open one of the harmonic left-hand thumb keys on the wing (Fig 26). Learning to cope with this self-imposed 'leak-factor' will not only teach us how to support more, but also demonstrate a more critically correct position on the reed for our lips (this will also serve to teach us how to cope with a real-world instrument not in peak condition).

Fig 26

- start by wedging open the high d″ key
- progress to the more challenging high c″ key.

6   Learn by trial and error the optimum embouchure setting for each note of the register by articulating

without the aid of the tongue; once this has been adopted, the note should speak punctually. Notice how the siting of the lips on the reed needs to be altered according to register – low register closer to the tip, high register closer to the wires – and also the variation in response between one note and another.

7   Since, according to the embouchure setting adopted, many fingerings can accidentally produce a pitch other than the note intended, we might learn how to avoid this phenomenon by deliberately exploring and then familiarizing ourselves with it.

- Fingering the low B♭' cause harmonics I to VII to sound. To help the right harmonic to speak, resort where necessary to 'half-holing' as indicated (Fig 27, next page).

- Utilising harmonic I to VII in turn, and starting each time on low B♭', explore the upward range obtainable on each, changing the half-holing as necessary (Fig 28).

- Produce a complete three-octave chromatic scale utilising harmonics I to VII, using the fingerings as shown (Fig 29).

8   Players of 'natural' brass instruments (i.e. those without valves) rely almost exclusively on their embouchure to select the register and move through the range of their instrument. While the bassoonist has keys to help him do this (especially those for the left hand thumb), embouchure and breath-leading skills should also play a crucial role, especially when slurring between intervals. We should strive to accommodate change of register with a subtle compensatory adjustment of breath-leading, minimizing the necessity for gross embouchure adjustment. The following three exercises target such demands; it is intended that the embouchure setting selected will accommodate an ever-widening range of register, encouraging our breath-leading

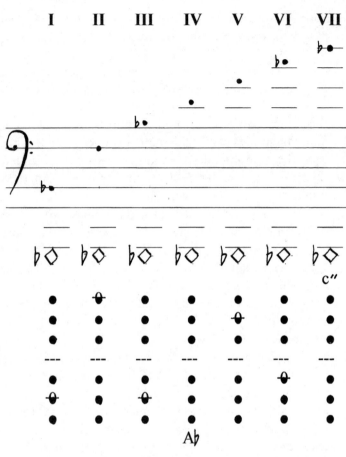

Fig 27

skills increasingly to develop as required. They also offer us the opportunity to observe how we are coping with these challenges whilst in action. Check in a mirror how much adjustment and modification of lip-on-reed position is visible. Initially we will have adopted different openings of jaw for each extreme of register; in time a wider setting will be unconsciously adopted which is equally valid for both extremes, while favouring neither: notice how much easier it is to

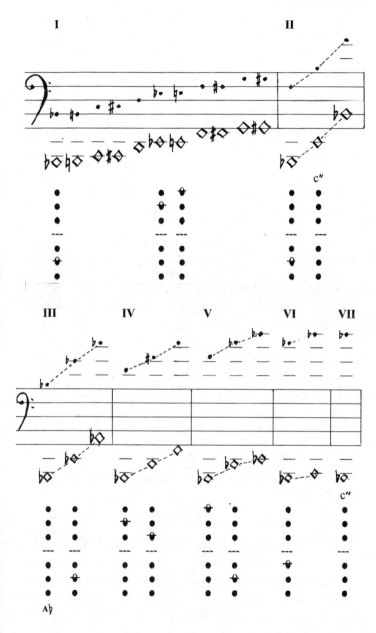

Fig 28

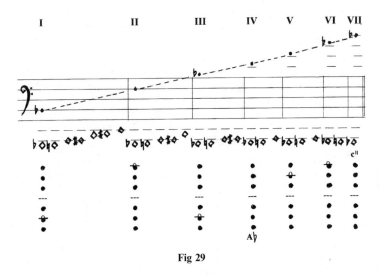

Fig 29

convert the embouchure setting from low register to high, than it is to do it in the opposite direction (Fig 30):

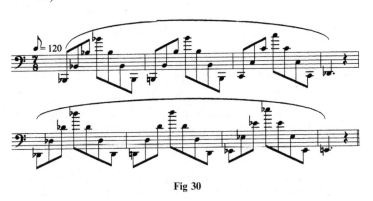

Fig 30

- This exercise in double-octave-intervals promotes the adoption of a single multi-purpose embouchure setting – flexible, and in the middle (Fig 31).
- This scale-in-octaves exercise will lessen our reliance on the whisper-key, a relatively modern device unavailable on the period instrument (Fig 32).

Fig 31

Fig 32

9 These exercises experiment creatively with some of the different factors involved with the embouchure;

a try first crowing with the reed on its own:
- changing the angle of the reed
- changing the amount of reed taken into the mouth
- changing the degree of jaw aperture (how open or closed the jaw)

b next repeat these three exercises, this time with both reed and crook

c finally repeat with the entire instrument, playing a sustained low C♯.

Notice how pitch, volume and resonance all change as we experiment creatively in this way. What we are striving for is to obtain by trial and error the desired pitch with the maximum intensity of signal per unit of effort.

107

10 Observe in a mirror the role played by the embouchure when controlling different and differing extremes of dynamic (Fig 33a, b, c, d):

Fig 33

11 We can flatten by up to a semitone the pitch of a note by progressively loosening the embouchure, playing at the extreme tip of the reed, and using extreme looseness of embouchure coupled with increased wind pressure; both the tip and aperture of the reed needs to be of sufficient width. This technique is useful for playing some of the low A′ passages that occur in Mahler's 4th Symphony (Fig 34):

Fig 34

Its use is also reported for playing the very exposed low B♮′ in Tschaikovsky's 5th Symphony by fingering C (daringly advocated by Prof. Valery Popov, Moscow) (Fig 35).

12 To develop our ability to play in the extreme high register whilst lessening the need for a tight embouchure and maintaining it relaxed (achieved by boosting abdominal support):

- whilst playing in this register, insert a pencil into the corner of the mouth without losing control
- instead of a pencil, ask a colleague to insert the tip of a finger
- instead of centring the reed in the middle of the lips to play, insert it well to the edge of the mouth.

Fig 35

4   Faults, Problems

Faults

- Embouchure efficiency is adversely affected by such playing syndromes as
  - faulty playing-position
  - unfavourable 'reed-angle-in-mouth'
  - deficient support and poor breath-leading skills
  - using reeds with a relatively high threshold of resistance.

  The fact that is perfectly possible for the player to tolerate and adapt to them – indeed to be unaware of the handicap that any might pose – does not alter this.

- Consider the classic comparison between the beginner with tight embouchure, stiff reed, flabby abdomen and small tone, contrasted with the expert with relaxed embouchure, responsive reed, firm abdominal support, and producing a carrying tone.

- An angle of reed entry unfavourable for maximising

109

embouchure efficiency: this remains the most common self-inflicted handicap for most players. While it cannot be denied that many manage to cope reasonably in spite of it, the removal of such a handicap would arguably confer such palpable benefits as greater responsiveness and an increased scope for adjusting intonation, dynamic, colour and intensity. The next most common handicap is excessive reed in the mouth.

- Some players pull a face before they play. While this might occasionally be necessary for oboists and trumpeters, the demands of our instrument are so different that we should not normally need to 'form' a special embouchure. Good breath support should enable us to adopt an embouchure which does not look artificial in any way.
- Retracting of the lower jaw to play has been advocated in America – perhaps in the hope that the resultant 'dampening' would produce a darker sound.
- The escaping of air from the sides of the mouth – a disturbing noise factor and irritating to colleagues – indicates excessive pressure applied by the jaw coupled with insufficient all-round lip control. The use of an over-resistant reed demanding greater air pressure will often cause this symptom. We should have the image of our embouchure functioning like the draw-string of a purse, with equalized 360° lip support, rather than a jaw-grip clamping from above and below like a carpenter's vice.
- A tight embouchure – the almost inevitable consequence of insufficient abdominal support – will tend to keep the jaws comparatively closed and throat tight, resulting in an impoverished tone quality. Building up the abdominal support will enable the embouchure to become more relaxed, allow the jaw to open, maximize the oral cavity and increase the tonal resonance.

Problems

The tiring of the embouchure through fatigue can cause the muscles momentarily to collapse. They can often be successfully resuscitated within the space of a few bars rest by 'palming'. This technique, also advocated for the treatment of eye-strain, consists of covering as much of the entire musculature as possible with the palm of the hand. This gentle contact by touch with the muscles in question helps them to relax and stimulates the blood supply to them. It is more effective than merely stopping in order to rest.

§4.6   Tongue / Articulation

1   Theory

Articulation literally means the jointing together of notes and groups of notes or phrases and how this is achieved. While for the string player the bow is responsible for initiating and terminating each note or phrase, on a wind instrument it is primarily the tongue. The ways articulation can be used make an important contribution to the musical expression. We need to develop awareness of the working of the tongue in order to train its obedience and develop the agility required for staccato.

Among all the woodwinds our instrument possesses a special capacity for the rendering of staccato. This important effect features in many of the solo passages written for the Classical Bassoon by Haydn, Mozart and Beethoven; the 19th century French instrument possessed a quality of dry, crisp staccato which was also capitalized upon by many composers. My teacher Archie Camden declared: "a good reliable staccato is one of the brightest jewels in the bassoon player's crown!" (Camden, 1961). However these days the German system bassoon has somewhat changed in character, being designed more for sonority and strength rather than the delivery of these effects. All too often today's playing styles are better suited to powerful expressiveness than to airy delicacy – delivering emphatic accents rather than light staccato. Nonetheless we must strive to achieve these articulation effects by the judicious choice of equipment and deployment of technique, so that we can do justice to them when they occur in the literature.

The most important skill required when playing with others – especially when standards are high – is the ability to begin a note punctually, without a bump, at the appropriate dynamic and in tune. The word most commonly in use for the starting of a note or phrase is 'attack'. This is unfortunate, as this seems to denote aggressiveness; more frequently we desire to make the note speak without accent or extraneous noise. Especially when the note is in the low register and soft, it is not only the setting of embouchure and breath support that is crucial, but the timing of tongue. The co-ordination of these requires practice.

When stopping a note, there are occasions when we wish to terminate it precisely – chopping it off cleanly as if it were a slice of salami. At other times a more artistic effect will be called for – allowing the sound to die away like the tail of a comet. For the former we may use the tongue, for the latter the breath.

Passages of notes are commonly articulated in various ways. Single tonguing is the most demanding; slurs, when introduced, break the monotony, while offering welcome respite for the tongue. Like every other set of muscles, the tongue is responsive to training; speed rates will increase if consistently practised over a period of days and weeks. The improvement curve will flatten in time; acquired skill will get lost if not maintained. The metronome is a useful monitor of performance and progress; keeping a written log to chart our progress will also be found a help. Every individual has scope for improvement, regardless of current ability. For some, progress will require more time and effort than it does for others; we should not be discouraged if others seem to be equipped with a more rapid tongue than we. It is fortunate for those of us with a sluggish tongue that double and triple tonguing (see below) can offer a reasonable substitute for single tonguing.

2   *Application*

We can start the note using either the tongue or merely the breath; we can also stop it using either method or a combination of both. Since there are undoubtedly occasions when it is desirable to use each of these techniques, they should all be mastered. They are described, compared and evaluated below.

Starting with Tongue

To play a note, having brought the instrument up into playing position we insert the reed between the lips and lightly place on it the tip of the tongue. It is judicious to have adopted a suitable playing position and crook design that presents the tip of the reed at that spot inside the mouth where the tongue may most conveniently reach it. Most authorities agree that the best spot on the tongue for reed contact is on the upper surface just behind the very tip. Having then closed the lips around the reed, we apply abdominal support from below in order to generate inside the mouth the pressure required for the note in question. With the requisite support of the lips around the reed and the correct fingering adopted, withdrawing the tongue frees the reed, admits the air, causes the blades to vibrate and the note to speak. The action of the tongue should give the note a clean and punctual start.

This remains the standard technique to employ.

Starting with Breath

We have already seen how we can verify the efficiency of embouchure and breath support for a given note by attempting to articulate it without the aid of the tongue. These two parameters need now to be more accurately judged than when tongued. Certain notes and certain fingerings will be found to respond better than others. Much will also depend on the relative readiness of the reed to vibrate. This method is often preferable for a sensitive, imperceptible entry.

This technique of articulating notes from the abdomen without using the tongue can be useful when extremes of either *pianissimo* or *sforzando* attack are required; an extreme high note will often speak more readily thus than when articulated with the tongue.

Double-dotted figures can be facilitated by articulating the rapid up-beat with the breath: *ta – huh | ta – huh | ta* rather than *ta – ta | ta – ta | ta*; this may be employed e.g. in the 6/8 passages in Borodin's *Polovtsian Dances* (Fig 36):

Fig 36

Stopping with Tongue

By replacing the tongue lightly back on the reed we stop the vibrating of the blades, controlling in this way the duration and termination of the note. With notes in rapid succession, it makes a short and rapid excursion away from the reed and back again. Care must be exercised taken not to allow the action of the tongue to chop off abruptly the end of a note or phrase. Its impact should not be violent like a cushion hitting a pole.

The most powerful benefit conferred is that we can maintain support and embouchure undisturbed throughout the entire duration of the breath, which is advantageous in a number of ways. By terminating a note in this manner, we are in position to sound the next pitch with the security of the same well-judged and undisturbed settings of lips, mouth and throat retained in place; the short note is enabled to share all the acoustic qualities of a long note, avoiding the risk of an undue proportion to noise to signal.

Its other principal benefit is to be able to deliver a really short, sharp staccato when required. It is also ideal for isolated notes. Here support must respond to register and dynamic: *staccatissimo* in *pianissimo* will require a very considerable degree of breath support, particularly in the low register.

'Soft tonguing' or legato-tonguing, in which the tongue interrupts only briefly or almost imperceptibly the sound, can be useful to help a treacherous slur to speak, to avoid a *portamento*, or to lend clarity and emphasis to a passage in legato.

Stopping with Breath

An alternative method of ending a note is to withdraw air-support from below so that the reed ceases to vibrate already before the tongue is replaced for the next 'attack'. Our abdominal muscles are now responsible for controlling the duration of the note. The collapse of pressure produces a reaction in both mouth and throat.

Compared with using the tongue this method avoids the risk of abruptness, while lending a pizzicato-like 'ring' to the sound. It matches well with the pizzicato cellos and basses in the Scherzo of Beethoven's Symphony No. 5 (Fig 37):

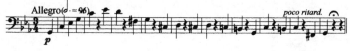

Fig 37

On the other hand where a 'French-type' of dry staccato is required in a resonant register, as in *The Sorcerer's Apprentice* of Dukas or in *Peer Gynt* of Grieg (Fig 38), it could be less successful:

Fig 38

Often the choice of which technique to employ will depend on the acoustics of the room.

Before the next note can be sounded, the tongue has to be positioned back on the reed and the process of preparation on the part of support and embouchure undertaken. If the new note or notes follow in too rapid succession, there is too little time for this to be accomplished accurately. In staccato passages, the collapse of pressure can produce a 'gobbling' reaction in the jaw. As a result the quality of tone and attack may suffer.

By comparison with the 'breath-stop' method, use of the tongue allows us to maintain the setting of abdominal support and embouchure undisturbed, making this the more efficient technique to adopt. We should think of a short note like a very small slice of cake which, in spite of its size, nevertheless contains its full complement of ingredients. Staccato notes on the bassoon should never sound like 'thuds' of impoverished tone quality and indeterminate pitch (where the noise factor predominates), but possess every attribute of a long note save that of duration. The method of using the tongue allows better for this. In certain modern scores, the duration of a note is precisely notated and needs to be accurately executed. Here the tongue will prove to be a more accurate time-keeper than the abdominal musculature; its use enables us to stop the sound cleanly.

In spite of such considerations however, all of these

techniques should be available to us as we may need to employ one in preference to another according to the requirements of the music and the acoustics of the room. It is my personal opinion that it is more efficient to use the tongue both to start and to stop each note or phrase, and it is this method that should be learned first.

A major challenge for every player is to execute rapid tonguing passages. The problems present themselves in different forms:

- Repetition of the same note. If the tongue can move lightly and freely at moderate speeds, we have a better chance of being able to train it to move ever faster. As we tongue more rapidly, we must try to involve only the tongue and not allow the jaw and throat to become involved or to tighten up.
- Moving passages requiring co-ordination of tongue and finger. When things go wrong, it is difficult to diagnose the cause; always check the fingers in *legato* first.
- Passages with intervals involving embouchure adjustment skills. As far as possible adopt a mid-point embouchure setting that will accommodate the extremes of range (see §4.5 Fig 31, p107).

In order for the note to speak punctually and without a 'bump', its preparation and timing must be properly carried out. It is helpful to think of a 'count-down' procedure to include the preparatory steps:

- adopting the fingering
- letting out the old, letting in the new breath
- taking the reed in the mouth and placing the tongue on the reed
- adopting the embouchure appropriate for the note in question
- applying the necessary breath support
- finally withdrawing the tongue to make the note speak.

The Bassoon

If the note fails to speak punctually, speaks with a bump, or even fails to speak at all, one or more of these steps must have been at fault in either timing or execution.

3 Routines

To school our control and awareness of the tongue's role in articulation, we first minimise our demands, as far as possible, then progressively increase the degree of challenge.

Tongue starts, Tongue stops

1   In order to school the obedience and responsiveness of the tongue in changing the duration of sound, think of the five differing note lengths given below in terms of different patterns of tongue movement, whereby the tongue alone is responsible for starting and stopping the note and thus varying the proportion of sound to silence. We practise first with the reed alone, in order to isolate the tongue from any sympathetic movement elsewhere and minimize the resistance that it encounters, then progressively adding the rest of the instrument without affecting its freedom and independence (Fig 39):

   • hold palm of hand over open mouth and apply abdominal pressure; reproduce the rhythmic patterns by withdrawing and replacing hand
   • tongue without actually blowing through the reed, checking with a mirror that the face and throat muscles remain uninvolved
   • now gently blow through the reed maintaining a constant pressure of breath behind the tongue with the abdominal muscles
   • blow hard enough to lightly crow the reed
   • repeat with crook added
   • with instrument, sounding a middle register note.

118

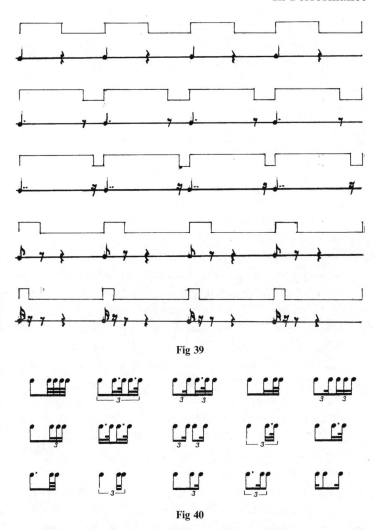

Fig 39

Fig 40

2   Train the tongue to execute different rhythms; each figure to be repeated eight times, and each at a progressively faster speed (Fig 40):

- crow reed alone
- now add the crook
- with instrument, sounding a middle register note
- follow with notes in low, and then in high register

119

3   Repetitive tonguing: concentrate on tongue efficiency by trying to visualize its brief journey and its point of reed contact, avoiding sympathetic involvement elsewhere (Fig 41):

Fig 41

- with just the reed on the crook, tonelessly
- now lightly crowed
- with instrument, on middle d.

4   Couple tonguing speed with repetition rate; the speed that our tongue can move is limited by the number of repetitions it has to undertake, which is in turn dependent on its stamina. In moving passages there is the additional problem of co-ordinating tongue and finger. Our embouchure must also respond to the differing pressure encountered when changing register. This purposely concise exercise, restricted to a mid-range of two octaves and allowing rests for recuperation, targets these challenges; as these become systematically increased, the speed may slow up accordingly (Fig 42).

5   To enhance staccato quality, add the note-length of demisemiquaver to the routines of Fig 39 (Fig 43). Try to improve quality and response in both single isolated tones and extended passages also in the high register (f′ up to d″) and the low register (F down to B♭′).

6   *Legato* tonguing: play a selected phrase so that it sounds *legato*, but tonguing each note – thus not allowing the separate articulation of each note to be detected. This requires that the tongue touches the reed only very rapidly and lightly.

Fig 42

Fig 43

Tongue starts, Breath stops

7   Repeat Fig 39, but now stop the sound with the breath rather than the tongue; follow with notes in low, and then in high register. Notice the different requirements now imposed by this technique.

Breath starts, Breath stops

8   Articulate notes throughout the register in *piano* with the breath alone. Foregoing the use of the tongue requires us to gauge accurately in advance the settings

121

of embouchure and breath support demanded by the note in question. Closing the eyes might help us to achieve the necessary concentration. Notice how the challenge to obtain a punctual response can vary from note to note. Notes in the low register will always be more difficult to attack in this way than high ones. The readiness of the note to speak will also depend to a certain extent on the readiness of the reed to vibrate.

4 Faults / Problems

Articulation

The tongue's task is made more difficult if the reed tip at which it is aiming is situated inside the mouth either too low down or too far back- that is, if the reed enters the mouth from a steep angle above, or if the player takes too much of it inside his lips. This is particularly the case where rapid and repeated strokes are concerned, and can be crucial for success in our ability to double-tongue (see below). Adopting a crook with a more user-friendly bend may resolve the former problem (see p96). With regard to the latter, though we may have begun with a good position, the reed has entered further into our mouth for the high register; now the articulation of the low register is hindered, because we have not consciously withdrawn it.

The location on the tongue of reed contact should not be too far back along the top, nor should it be on the underside of the tongue.

With regard to looking for ways to resolve problems of articulation the example of Demosthenes may be cited. This famous Greek orator cured himself of a speech impediment by forcing himself to declaim initially with a pebble in his mouth; having to overcome this self-imposed handicap evidently succeeded in eradicating the problem. A similar teaching technique has been endorsed by a clarinettist colleague.

Quality of Staccato

Our attempts at staccato will sound stodgy and insufficiently crisp – failing to match that of the oboe, for example – unless we remain constantly aware of the demands involved. In most circumstances, to achieve and maintain a really spiky staccato requires deliberate effort. The shorter the staccato, not only does the tongue have to be faster, but the air support has to be greater in order to activate the reed-blades.

While separating notes with breath rather than tongue, a glance in the mirror will sometimes reveal considerable jaw involvement;. The momentary opening and closing of our lower jaw may be in response to the change of pressure inside the mouth once the support is switched off; however it is more likely to betray an involuntary 'gobbling' with the jaw in sympathy with the activity of the tongue. Ideally the style of reed we use, and the control point on the blades adopted by the lips (i.e. how close they are to the wires) should not require that the support applied by the lips needs supplementing by upward pressure from the lower jaw.

In the attack of a note and especially in staccato, the most common fault is that the start is marred by a noise factor – sometimes referred to as 'cracking'. This problem can – indeed should – be solved by the adoption of safer fingerings, such as the conscientious use of 'harmonic' keys. However this risk is considerably reduced when the setting of support and embouchure corresponds to the demands of the pitch in question. When these settings are disturbed by terminating the note with breath rather than tongue, care needs to be taken to re-set them accurately.

Speed of Tongue

It is axiomatic that maximum speed will only be achieved if and when there is little muscular involvement elsewhere. This can only be by keeping loose and free – 'relaxed' – whilst certain muscles are having to work very hard.

5   *Alternative Tonguing Techniques*

Double tonguing

This technique, long common on the flute, has often in the past been considered impossible on the bassoon. However by now most competent players have mastered it. In learning how to do it, the first step is to have a clear picture of what we are asking our tongue to do. Try saying, but without voicing, the syllables *tut-tut-tut*, holding the palm of the hand just in front of the lips. We will sense how the impact of breath is punctuated by the tip of the tongue rebounding from behind the upper teeth back to a mid-air spot within the middle of the mouth. Now repeat, saying instead the syllables *kuk-kuk-kuk*, using this time the back of the tongue against the soft palate. In each case it is a part of the tongue that interrupts the flow of breath through the lips. If we now try speaking the syllables *tuku-tuku-tuku*, we will observe how the flow of breath is alternately shut off by first the tip and then the back of the tongue.

Slow practising with only the reed in the mouth will help us to aim the tip of the tongue accurately back on to the reed when making the *kut* stroke. Note that, if when playing the reed-tip is presented to the tongue too far inside the mouth or too low down, the technique may not be found possible (see below). We may then try slowly with the whole instrument. We must only increase the speed gradually so that we always maintain evenness and control, curbing any tendency for the tongue to run away. In time the quality and evenness of the staccato notes should improve, so that at slow speeds it is barely distinguishable from single tonguing. A word of warning: working at double tonguing should not cause us to neglect the acquisition of as rapid a single tonguing technique as possible. In some comservatoires students are not allowed to use it until their senior year.

A common reason why some players are unable to learn this technique is that they are presenting the tip of the reed at a location in the mouth which is unfavourable for the tongue. When we ask the tongue to execute as sophisticated a manoeuvre as a repeated ricochet back and forth in the mouth, we must ensure that the reed-tip is within its reach – situated in the position which is right for it (see §4.5)

Routines for practising double tonguing:

1   with reed alone in the mouth, practise both *tk-tk-tk-tk* and *kt-kt-kt-kt* tongue strokes at a comfortable speed, but noiselessly in order to concentrate on the action of the tongue
2   repeat, but now lightly crowing the reed; guard against involuntary tightening of the embouchure
3   taking now the instrument in the left hand and a metronome in the right, play repeated notes at a comfortable speed (Fig 44):

Fig 44

4   repeat, adopting the progressively slower speeds of 108, 100 and 92
5   repeat, now adopting the progressively faster speeds of 120, 126, 132, 138 and 144.

Triple tonguing
There are three varieties: *tkt-ktk*, *tkt-tkt*, and *ttk-ttk* – of which the first is probably the easiest and most useful. We should practise the first of these by initially using the back, rather than the tip of the tongue to articulate – *k-k-k* tongue strokes, rather than *t-t-t*.

The Bassoon

Flutter tonguing
Practise by causing the tip of the tongue to oscillate close
behind the front teeth, as when rolling an *r*, and try to
maintain this motion whilst playing.

Slap tongue
A similar effect to that commonly used by jazz sax-
ophonists may be produced on the bassoon when, whilst
fingering a low note and supporting with the breath, the
tongue repeatedly 'slaps' the tip of the reed.

Vertical and lateral tonguing
With a little practice, the tongue can be induced to move
up and down vertically from the tip of the reed; this will be
found to produce a rapid feathery effect. A lateral technique, where the tip of the tongue moved across the reed
horizontally from side to side, was reportedly used successfully by the Italian clarinettist Carlo Luberti (1885-?);
its advantage lay in enhanced rapidity and "the lesser
energy with which the vibrating column of air is inter-
rupted, thereby obtaining an almost continuous sounding
of the note by the tongue" (Pace, 1943).

§4.7   Fingers / Finger Technique

Here it is finger technique and our fingers that are considered, rather than fingering and the choosing of fingerings (for which see §4.8).

1   Theory

The bassoon, alone among woodwind instruments,
employs every finger. These hardly share an equal level of
ability, certain being weaker and more sluggish than others

(although all can become more strong and agile through practice). Most have more than just a tone-hole or single key to manage, the left thumb alone having eight or nine keys under its control. In the upper register the fingerings lack system and are hardly intuitive, because of the complex acoustics imposed by the lattice of tone-holes (see §4.8 *Acoustics*). All of this makes finger technique on bassoon arguably more difficult than on either flute, clarinet or saxophone. Independence and co-ordination of the fingers is called for; pianists, especially those whose fingers have been schooled by finger exercises such as those by Brahms and Dohnányi, will be at a distinct advantage here.

When we play, and especially when we sight-read, we rely at the moment of performance on the ability of our fingers to respond to the instructions given. Once the brain has comprehended and processed the task at hand, the fingers have to execute a range of complicated movements. They can only do this in so far as they have been pre-programmed with the skills and reflexes to perform reliably without supervision.

The traditional method for teaching finger technique is by means of **Scale and Arpeggio** and of **Etude**. Both methods however call for common sense in how they are applied and are often too limited in their scope; certain modifications are proposed here.

Scale and Arpeggio

In tonal music our fingers have to navigate within well-defined limits – the seven common to the key in question out of the twelve chromatic notes available. A good way of training them to do this is by practising scales and arpeggios, given that most passages consist of sequences of notes forming part of these. Thus for each key, be it major or minor, the brain and fingers will be programmed with the necessary skills to execute what can be quite complex juxtapositions of fingerings. However the conventional forms generally used have shortcomings.

Fig 45

- ditty-like formulas such as Fig 45 are insufficiently relevant to their main purpose; the extremities of range beyond each key-note must always be included, since this is where the technical demands are at their most severe, while the turn-around at the top of the scale can present special problems that are not relevant here
- scale patterns are usually restricted to those that are diatonic and in thirds.

The main purpose of learning scales and arpeggios is, for tonal music, to furnish brain and finger with the reflex skills to handle every conceivable pattern peculiar to the twelve keys. To do this, they must not only cover the entire working range, but should also cover intervals beyond the third up to the octave; once the selection of seven tones has been made, re-deploying them in other patterns will be found less problematic than it might seem at first sight. Furthermore, given the demands of modern music, similar scales in chromatic intervals should also be included. While each scale has to be practised in both directions, we need only pursue one direction at a time. In *legato*, other useful purposes are served:

- at faster speeds the fingers learn fluency and evenness
- at slower speeds the intervals can be checked for intonation and cleanliness
- we learn to identify those intervals requiring greater care or special fingerings

- as scale intervals become wider, both embouchure and breath-leading will, by having new demands to satisfy, be taught a number of valuable skills.

Etude

The etude is a mechanism designed to present us with other technical problems not covered by scale or arpeggio. While early *Caprices* presented technical study-material attractively enough to be suitable for public performance (such as the sets by Gebauer and Jacobi), most etudes written over the last 150 years are too dreary musically to qualify for this. To be worthwhile, an etude should requite us for the time and trouble spent mastering it; this is best done by concentrating on specific problems that should be obvious at first glance – and ideally spelled out as superscript.* Most etudes written for bassoon are too diffuse in their subject matter; they are both arbitrary in how they treat the technical problems they select, and rarely successful in a pill-sweetening attempt to be attractive musically. When employed, etudes should be carefully selected, each with a specific end in view.

Routine

The routines given in this book are designed to supplement etudes – if not largely to supplant them; their advantages include:

- offering a better return per investment of time and effort
- concentrated, targeting no more than one topic at a time
- concise, free of superfluities and systematic in coverage
- adaptable to specific requirement.

* as in Julius Weissenborn (ed. Waterhouse): *Fagott-Studien op. 8/2*, Universal Fagott Edition, Wien 1985.

Accepting that we are creatures of habit, we should guard against mistakes, avoiding them as far as possible. Thus our adopted practice speed should never exceed one thought likely to allow for playing without mistake. The repetition of a mistake will tend only to consolidate what is a faulty procedure, thereby making it more difficult to eradicate later on. When it is our fingers that have caused the mistake, it is better to stop and analyse where, how and why it happened, rather than endlessly repeat it in the hope that it will rectify itself.

The patterns of *legato* scales in diatonic and chromatic intervals given below train the fingers to cope with a comprehensive range of eventualities; other benefits conferred include:

- we will learn which are those intervals that in *legato* require especial care and how to slur between them
- managing wide intervals will help to maintain an equalized embouchure setting (i.e. one favouring neither extreme) and an open jaw.

2   Application

Because five of the fingers cover open tone-holes, the pads of these fingers need to develop a sensitive awareness in order to ensure that they seal the fingerholes completely. This awareness is especially necessary for the left-hand index finger, as this is the one responsible for the technique of 'half-holing' (see §4.8). This is achieved by uncovering the top finger-hole by whatever amount is required by the fingering in question. The best way to do this is by rotating the finger, rather than retracting it.

For the extreme low notes, players with large hands often find it a good idea to crook the thumb at right angles to play the C and to keep it in this position for the B♮′

touch using the knuckle; the B♭′ touch can then be depressed by merely straightening the thumb. In this way the base of the index finger remains in contact with the instrument all of the time, avoiding any risk of the fingers coming off the tone-holes: also the thumb does not have to move so far away from its normal area of activity and this helps its speed and mobility.

The left thumb has other problems to cope with when having to move rapidly between the crook key and the three or four adjacent keys. This can often involve passing over the c♯ key touch without depressing it, which demands that we momentarily release the pressure of the thumb. The relative heights of these may be individually adjusted in order to facilitate matters.

If the girth of the long joint is small, as with some old instruments, and if the player's hand is large, it sometimes helps to build up with a curved layer of cork the spot where the base joint of the index finger rests on the instrument (see §3.2).

It is evident that greater ease and speed of finger movements will be achieved if unnecessary movement of the hands and fingers is avoided. Fingers need not travel away from the tone-holes and key-touches more than the minimum; in this way they will find the way back surer and quicker. The fingers of an expert player only move a minimal distance.

Rollers can facilitate and speed up the journey that the fingers have to make between keys. However these are not used by every player; if the key touches are well designed, their absence will not be missed (see §3.2).

When trilling, especially when more than one finger is involved, greater speed and looseness can be achieved if more than just the finger in question is involved: e.g. if the entire wrist is rotated when trilling A♭-B♭; here the hand rest should not inhibit the freedom of the right hand fingers.

The Bassoon

The perfect execution of a passage requires that the contribution of finger, tongue and breath – and usually of embouchure as well – be of impeccable standard. When practising, it is the contribution of the fingers that should first be checked. Practise fingers alone without blowing, concentrating on this aspect free from other distractions. Observe them working both directly and in a mirror. Only incorporate the other skills when satisfied that the performance of the fingers can be relied on.

Scales and arpeggios are best practised from memory. Closing of the eyes, by removing any possible source of distraction, will aid concentration. While many of the more difficult routines would pose an excessive challenge to the memory, and are thus better practised from the music, the simpler diatonic forms should be committed to memory. Regarding range, the upper watershed of top c″ should be crossed in order to gain experience of the extra demands encountered beyond this note. They are best played in *legato*, so as to train in slurring and embouchure skills and help finger-error to be detected. The speed selected should be that commensurate with reasonable accuracy, the rhythm inexorable, with wrong notes callously ignored rather than permitted to disturb it; the pace adopted need not be rigidly consistent throughout – to maintain a consistent degree of challenge, parts of the same scale may be taken faster or slower.

3 Routines

1 Assess and compare the relative agility of the ten fingers:
   - finger low E♭; then without playing trill each finger one after the other
   - play this succession of ten trills (Fig 46):

Fig 46

2   Given that demands on finger technique are greatest in the upper register, more intensive scale practice is required here than in other parts of the range. This routine, repeated in all major keys by supplying appropriate key-signatures, systematically covers every pair of juxtaposed fingerings (some requiring non-intuitive digital manoeuvres). It should be practised first at slow speed in double dotted rhythm. Taken at speed, it can prove a useful warm-up exercise (Fig 47):

Fig 47

3   Programming finger skills employed in tonal music, this scale routine includes every diatonic interval from second to octave; features include:

●   notation without key-signature and in white notes, enabling them to be read in any of the 12 major or harmonic minor keys and grouped in alternative rhythms (groups of three, four etc.)

●   the entire working range of each key is covered

●   each scale pursues one direction only

●   the first of each pair starts in descent (rather than at the bottom), as this will be found to facilitate matters as the size of interval progressively increases.

To be practised *sempre legato*, to be accented first in groups of two, and later of three and four (Fig 48a/b):

133

The Bassoon

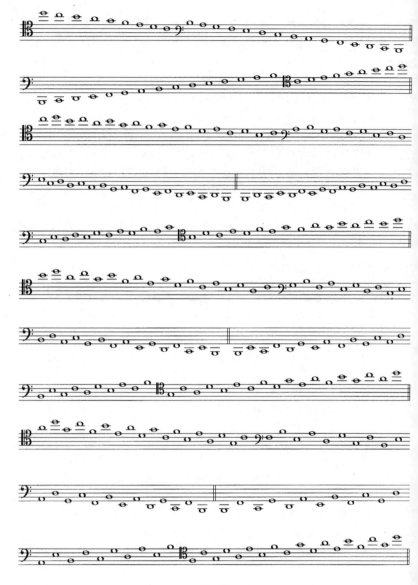

Fig 48a

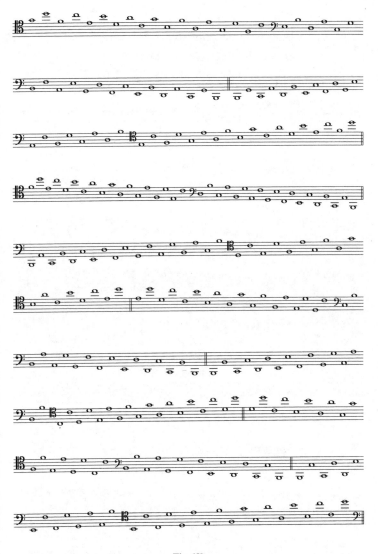

Fig 48b

4 Designed on similar principles to **3**, this routine of scales in chromatic intervals will prepare for the technical demands of atonal music by including every

135

diatonic interval from second to octave; every conceivable slur, every conceivable juxtaposition of finger
position is systematically covered; *legato*, to be accented in groups of two, and later of three (Fig 49a/d):

Fig 49a

Fig 49b

Fig 49c

Fig 49d

5   Arpeggio routine: a) twelve major, b) twelve minor, c) twelve dominant sevenths and d) three diminished sevenths; *legato*, to be accented in groups of three (Fig 50):

Fig 50

4   Faults / problems

The fingers should be maintained flexible and as free of
tension as possible. This will be easier to achieve if they are
kept lightly curved as opposed to straight.

The lifting of fingers a long way off the hole or key is to
be avoided; this will also help to avoid extraneous noise.

Some support systems impose more weight on the left
forearm than others. When this results in the left hand
having to bear too much of the weight of the instrument,
the fingers are not free to move easily. The more evenly
that the weight can be distributed between the two arms the
better.

The hand-rest fitted on the butt should assist the fingers
of the right hand in the execution of technical passages. It
should give support where needed to the wrist and arm
without interfering with them (see §3.2). When the hand-
rest is unsuitable it can also hamper the mobility of the
thumb and index-finger. This will often be the case unless it
has been chosen carefully, or custom-built to suit the
individual.

§4.8   Fingerings / Acoustics

1   Fingerings

For much of the range the standard fingerings in universal
use seem rational in the way they function. However in the
upper part of the register they become complex and non-
intuitive, adjacent tones sometimes requiring unrelated
combinations of fingers. This is due to the complex
acoustics of the instrument, primarily the role played by
the 'extension tube' and the tone-hole lattice it imposes (see
below). Instruments can vary in their response to fingerings
– both according to workshop, between instruments from
the same workshop, between different crooks, and even
between different reeds. Whilst in recent years makers have

been successful in producing instruments with a high level of consistency, in the past most players have had to adopt personal fingerings in order to humour particular notes on their own particular instrument.

For many of the higher notes a number of alternative fingerings are usually possible. Different players will often prefer different fingerings on the same instrument (usually the ones they are used to!). All this explains why printed fingering charts often fail to correspond with each other in the upper register.

The table of 'fingered harmonics' (see Fig 27, p104) will already have indicated how many of our fingerings may have been derived, when they are a contrived harmonic produced from a basic fingering. Making use of these same principles we can possibly discover fresh fingerings for ourselves.

In order to guarantee safety of attack of the middle-register notes from f♯ to c′, which are fingered in the same way as at one octave lower, it is necessary to use **a**) 'half-holing' and **b**) 'flicking' techniques:

a 'Half-hole technique' refers to the partial opening of a tone-hole – usually the uppermost left-hand index finger – and can vary from an appreciable amount for middle f♯ to a tiny chink for g♯′. "It is important to match whenever possible the size of the tone-hole opening to the acoustical requirements of the note being played, since the reliability of response, intonation and stability is critically related to this *[...]* Since both the whisper key and the half-hole functions act independently as register or octave vents, they have a cancelling effect when incorrectly used together. As a general rule, therefore, whenever mechanically possible, the whisper vent should not be open when the first tone hole is partially open." (Cooper & Toplansky, 1968).

b 'Flick keys' – thumb harmonic keys, when used to ensure the safe attack of the upper octave of basic fingerings – should be used conscientiously in scale practice. Fig 51 identifies which notes benefit from which key. A momentary opening of the harmonic hole needs to coincide with the sounding of the note in question to avoid obtrusion of the lower harmonic (known as 'cracking' or 'clucking'). To achieve this the tip of the thumb, held poised above in readiness, is swept downwards to give a 'swipe' at the harmonic key (a glancing blow is more efficient than simply moving it down and up). There are occasions, such as in rapid passage work, when their use can often be dispensed with, but there are so many combinations of notes where their use is necessary in order to avoid 'clucking' that it is advisable to get early into the habit of using them. Although the use of these keys is traditional in Europe, it has been far from universal in the U.S., a problem that has caused some controversy (Fig 51):

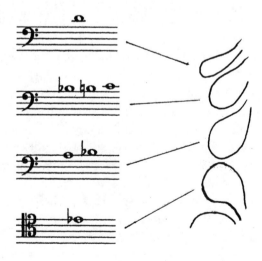

Fig 51

The Bassoon

It is a puzzling phenomenon that both player and instrument seem to have a surprising capacity to learn improved response from a strange fingering. For example, the beginner will often have adopted a fingering peculiar to himself for a certain note. When given the standard fingering, the result will sound markedly inferior at first; however practice will usually make perfect – as if both instrument and player have learnt the necessary knack of how to achieve improved response.

It is best for the beginner to learn to use standard fingerings: these will then remain serviceable if and when he changes to another instrument. Teachers should teach their students these standard fingerings, rather than any idiosyncratic fingerings of their own. These basic fingerings should be simple, involving as few fingers as possible so as to facilitate technique – fingerings for the bassoonist are complex enough as it is – i.e. they need not involve too much the use of auxiliary keys (see below). This basic 'vocabulary' of fingerings will consist of those that the player resorts to instinctively when sight reading and in technical passages. To avoid confusion, it is unwise except where absolutely necessary to use too many alternative fingerings. While it is common for students of the French system *basson* to learn one set of fingerings for 'tone' and another for 'technique' (see Allard, 1975), it should be possible to avoid this on the German instrument. A few notes, like middle e♭ and upper f', usually need to be 'vented', that is, opening an auxiliary key in addition to the basic fingering in order to boost sonority; these include exposed sustained notes held loud or soft, when they need tuning sharp or flat, or for *pianissimo* attack.

Many players vent with the low E♭ key the entire upper register (from e' to c''), notes that seem to gain in tone quality and strength when a hole further down the bore is opened or closed. . "Its more frequent use is as a resonance key. *[...]* It will usually improve the tone quality, intonation, and stability *[...]* For the most part, this key should be considered as an integral part of the fingering and incorporated into the bassoonist's basic technique." (Cooper & Toplansky, 1968). However it needs to be pointed out that what may be gratifying to the player (especially if the hole to be opened is one of those closest to his own ear) is usually much less noticeable to the listener. We must ask if the effort involved in engaging extra finger(s) for these notes is worth it, given the fact that most bassoon fingerings are complex enough as it is.

The criteria for adopting a fingering should be:

- that the note is in tune at all dynamic levels, especially with adjacent notes
- that it should match them tonally
- that the tone quality of the note should be good – i.e. that a representative spread of overtones should be present
- that it allows for good projection in both very quiet and very loud playing
- that it offers as little resistance to the player as possible
- that it involves as few fingers as possible.

Over a period of years, most players decide to replace an old fingering, that for one reason or another is no longer serviceable, with a new fingering. These are best inculcated by practising scales and arpeggios whilst taking deliberate care to observe them conscientiously.

It is dangerous to rely too readily on a specially adopted fingering to help resolve a particular problem. Keys or fingers are sometimes added:

- to mute or deaden an otherwise too lively sound, with the object of making it speak more softly
- to sustain a note up to pitch
- to strengthen the sonority of a weak and lifeless note.

However such corrections are often better made by modifying the support offered by embouchure and breath – in other words to rely on ourselves to control and master the instrument. We should use fingerings which respond well to the way we play and which allow us scope for nuance and flexibility. This will be safer and more satisfying to us in the long term.

This is not to deny that some notes will always require humouring. Notes such as middle e♭, middle g and tenor f♯′ are problem notes on many instruments – especially older ones. Makers have argued in the past that if we try to improve these notes by altering the instrument we risk creating bigger problems in other areas.

'Fake' fingerings are simplified versions of the standard fingerings. When it comes to trills, special fake fingerings often have to be used. Similarly, there is a temptation to find fake fingerings for certain florid melodic solos in the upper register in order to make them easier. However this should only be done exceptionally, for these reasons:

- in the stress of the moment, it is easy to forget what has been learned specially for the occasion
- faked notes often sound inferior
- when sight-reading, the less alternative fingerings habitually in use, the less confusion will there be at subconscious levels of awareness
- time and effort spent practising with standard fingerings will benefit our technique in general.

Nonetheless the player will come across passages in time when fake fingerings are called for: they should be copied into a notebook and kept for reference.

Where the instrument offers a choice of key for a note (F♯, G♯ and B♭ keys on the butt) we should familiarize ourselves with both alternatives. There will inevitably be occasions when they need to be used, and we will then be able to use them without hesitation.

146

Extreme high notes can pose special problems. It is a fact of the orchestral bassoonist's life that modern composers persist in using them – e.g. e″ by Schoenberg (*Variationen* op.31) and Ravel (*Concerto pour piano*), f″ by Berg (*Wozzeck*) and Françaix (*Sérénade*). Earlier players coped by using special crooks and harder reeds; nowadays many have high-note keys fitted on the wing joint. However not everyone finds such expedients to be necessary; to persuade these high harmonics to speak, it is primarily the pressure of breath, rather than of lip, that needs to be stepped up. Obtaining them is a knack which comes with experience, relying more on nice judgment than brute force.

Next page (Fig 52) is a table of suggested fingerings that deal with:

a high notes **b** trills **c** projection
d technical facility **e** intonation

2   Acoustics

If we compare the 'tone-hole lattice' – the pattern of tone-hole distribution throughout the bore – of the bassoon with that of an instrument like the Boehm-system flute, it is clear that the latter's uniformity of spacing / size of tone-hole and of wall-thickness will tend to produce less problematic fingering patterns. In the case of the bassoon, such design features as:

- uneven conicalness of bore
- irregular distribution and spacing of tone-holes throughout the bore
- lack of gradation of tone-hole size
- irregular and inconsistent depth of the tone-hole chimneys

inevitably lead to a system of fingering that lacks logic, consistency and intuitiveness.

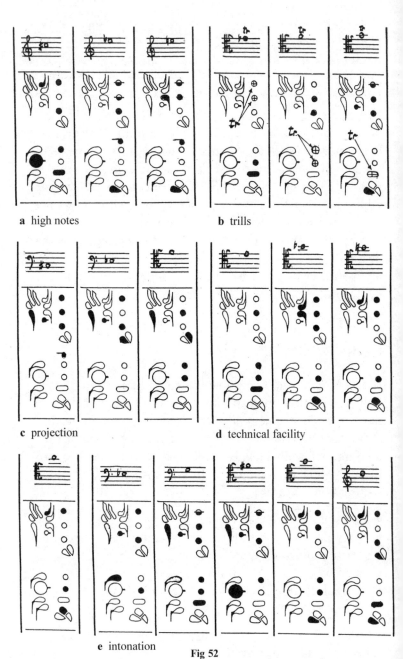

a high notes

b trills

c projection

d technical facility

e intonation

Fig 52

The crook is a component that affects the acoustics of the entire instrument. Together with the reed, it forms the apex of the entire cone and must match the acoustic needs of the rest of the instrument. Because the role played by the bore is more critical the closer it is to the sound generator, this lends it thus a special importance (see also §3.2 *Crook*).

Efforts have been made in the past to iron out and remove such inconsistencies; 'reform models' designed in the mid 19th century by followers of Boehm were considered at the time to be damaging to the essential tone character of the instrument. Neither they, nor the last serious attempt at a *Reformfagott* – Kruspe's genial model patented in 1893 (Pl 7e) – proved to be commercially successful.

§4.9   *Avant-garde* Techniques

Innovative playing techniques have been developed in recent years applied to almost every instrument forming, together with aleatorics and electronics, part of the 'New Music' trends developed during the 1950s. Many of these were identified by Bruno Bartolozzi in his book *New Sounds for Woodwind* (1982), which the author categorized into monophonic and multiphonic effects. The bassoon lends itself better than its fellow woodwinds to many of these effects because of the properties of its acoustic and reed; his chief adviser was the bassoonist Sergio Penazzi (*d* ca1980), whose *Metodo per fagotto* (1972) and *Il fagotto: altre tecniche* (1982) give fingerings for quarter and multiple tones and describe the necessary adjustments to embouchure. The *Systematik* (1988) by Heinz Riedelbauch also deals exhaustively with the subject.

In 1985 the East Berlin bassoonist Dieter Hähnchen published an album of 17 specially commissioned compositions for solo bassoon: *Zeitgenössische Musik für Fagott solo*. Almost all of them employ these and other techniques, the notation and execution of which is fully described and explained in a useful appendix in German and English.

While all of these concern themselves with the German bassoon, *Actuellement le basson: traité pratique des nouvelles techniques au basson* by Alexandre Ouzounoff (1986) relates to the French system instrument.

Innovative techniques called for in recent times include:

- micro-intervals (also incorporating *glissando*)
- multiphonics (split tones)
- harmonics
- fingerings to produce alternative tone-colours (dark, bright)
- the use of extreme high notes
- the use of a mute
- key percussion effects (key noise)
- 'disjointed instrument' effects (playing reed only, crook only, reed + crook and so on)
- alternative kinds of staccato – hard, soft, *cuivré* (metallic), on reed without blowing etc
- flutter tongue
- rotary breathing (see §4.4 *Other*).

Some new works incorporate music-theatre effects. The version of *In Freundschaft* by Karlheinz Stockhausen for bassoon solo (1983) is directed to be played on stage in costume from memory with choreographed movements. The *Sonata abassoonata* by P.D.Q. Bach (*alias* Peter Schickele) (1996) for bassoon and piano requires the performer to play both instruments simultaneously.

Electronic effects obtained by the use of close-contact microphones, applied to the instrument to amplify and modify the tone, are used especially by jazz musicians. Other works feature computer interacting dynamically with player.

§4.10   Brain / Interpretation / Memory

Brain

It remains for us to consider the participation of the brain in performance. Other related topics are discussed under §4.11 and §4.13.

Whilst **performing**, the role of our brain is:

- to establish and maintain tempo and pace (in the absence of a conductor), and to designate phrasing, agogic, and all other matters relating to active interpretation
- to check our efforts whilst in action, and to actively steer those playing techniques requiring deliberate attention at the time
- to process intellectually the musical text and programme our responses to the music as it unfolds
- when playing from memory, to take over from the eyes their task in apprehending of the text.

Whilst **practising**, the brain's role is:

- to plan the schedule of work requiring to be done; if we are taking regular lessons, such decisions should have been made for us by our teacher – who should also have given guidance on how and what to practise, depending on the syllabus in use
- to check attentively and assess what is actually coming out of the instrument (as opposed to what we think ought to be coming out), detecting mistakes and diagnosing other shortcomings as they occur
- to plan and implement suitable remedial measures to deal with such problems. We should take an interest in the psychology of making mistakes. Wherein lies the blame for the wrong note? If caused by a lapse of the fingers, rather than for any other reason, have they

nonetheless been carrying out orders, but – due to a misunderstanding somewhere along the line of command – issued with the wrong orders? If this is the case, it is this misunderstanding which must first be identified and rectified – *comprendre, c'est tout pardonner* ...

While at the actual moment of performance we are, to a large extent, dependent on 'automatic-pilot', we nonetheless place great reliance on the brain. Its task should resemble that of the trainer watching his team from the touch-line; uninvolved personally in the action, he is able to assess objectively the performance of his players. Thus we need to remain objectively in control, without losing perspective by becoming immersed in practicalities. For the finished result, many technical processes may require simultaneous supervision in order for them to be performed adequately. At the same time from an interpretation point of view the unfolding progress of the music has to be monitored. For this we must both exercise intellectual grasp and a capacity to externalize emotion and feeling. Can we afford the agogic we use to be exclusively instinctive – or does it need at certain times to be deliberately contrived?

Interpretation

In performance, the interpretation we give to the music should not rely merely on the brain, but rather on both heart and mind – a combination of artistic instinct tempered by intellectual control. Each has an important role to play. The best interpretation we can give will be one that totally reflects our individual qualities of musicianship and to which our artistic personality has responded to the music as completely as possible. Sheer technical perfection – though a useful pre-requisite – is not enough. As well as the brain, our emotions and feelings have a crucial role to play by responding as we perform. Our emotional response to the music we are playing will heighten the expressiveness of our performance and what it means to our listeners. Our emotions and feelings are precious sensibilities – though fragile. But while sensitivity is to be nurtured and cherished, it also needs to be kept under a degree of objective supervision, lest we lose control of our interpretation by letting emotion unduly take over. At worst we may even run the risk of having a nervous breakdown, if our system is insufficiently robust to cope with the stressful demands made on it.

Listening to a work well-known to us, hearing it performed by different artists will demonstrate the scope for interpretation of the individual performer. To compare performances by poor or mediocre artists with those that are excellent is both amusing and instructive; the differences of conception and interpretation correspond to the strengths possessed by each. It will also demonstrate what is needed to engage our attention and offer us an artistic experience.

A meaningful performance calls for more than a mere playing of the notes. This can be demonstrated by listening to a child recite a text – such as a poem or a bible passage – the meaning of which he or she does not fully comprehend. Even if the words are correctly pronounced, for it to be made intelligible and interesting, their meaning has to have been understood, otherwise the result may well degenerate into a banal rigmarole. However once having understood their sense, the meaning will be put across by the idiomatic use of tone of voice, accentuation, timing and choice of breath spots. This analogy can be applied also to the performance of a piece of music. This arguably illustrates the importance of processing intellectually (and let us hope sympathizing with) the music we play in order to interpret it meaningfully for our listeners.

An insufficient degree of acquaintance with the music means that we have to concentrate too much of our attention on reading the text. This will distract us from more important considerations and absorb valuable attention and awareness that might be better used elsewhere. It can also mean that we have failed to process it intellectually. Committing it to memory entails its consideration on many levels and ensures that we become thoroughly acquainted with it (see below). However for those for whom learning and performing repertoire from memory will be uncharted territory, it remains important to incorporate as many of these benefits as possible.

To arrive at an 'interpretation' of period music, practical decisions are necessary – dependant on the style of the music – relating to:

- tempo: our choice of basic speed should be well judged, taking into consideration such objective factors as the complexity of the music's texture and the room acoustic. Regarding the altering of tempo within a movement, hard and fast rules hardly apply, except to observe that the mechanical rigour of many of today's performances is a modern phenomenon
- agogic: liberties of time taken with the unfolding of a phrase – is a matter of personal taste; it is often more effective to recover any time lost through the taking of such liberties rather than that tempo should drag
- *rubato*: in Hans Richter's memorable words: "Sir, rubato, a little, then and now, yes! But always, my God, never!"*
- dynamics: note that the insertion of gratuitous 'echo' effects is hardly stylish
- articulations: historic models, often remarkable for their diversity and inventiveness, should be studied

* quoted in Camden, 1961, p51.

- ornamentation: consult historic models, as to degree and nature
- cadenzas and lead-ins
- trills, whether to start on upper note, with or without *Nachschlag* (turn) etc
- execution of appoggiaturas – whether on or before beat, long/short etc
- *vibrato*: consider rather as ornament.

Golden rule: consult the score, having first ensured that it is reliable.

Performing a work for unaccompanied instrument poses special challenges. Here the soloist foregoes every support given by an accompaniment, such as helping the listener comprehend matters of tonality and metre. It is instructive to listen to performances of works for other unaccompanied instruments in order to realise the problem. In the case of a tonal piece, the opening bars must be played in such a way as to enable the listener to grasp the time-signature, locate the down-beat and identify the tonality. It will be dangerous to indulge in too much *rubato* and agogic until he has been made to feel thoroughly orientated.

Memory

An actor on stage can hardly characterize his role convincingly until he can dispense with reading from the text. The committing of a piece to memory ensures that we have become thoroughly acquainted with it on many levels and are able to interpret it with spontaneity (especially passages in *recitativo* style and cadenzas). It is thus arguably a worthwhile investment of time and trouble.

My own experience serving on competition juries has convinced me that those who perform from memory consistently outplay the others. It might be argued that those

with this capacity and confidence must also possess
superior abilities in other directions, and that only such
competitors would face the added risks entailed by having
to rely exclusively on memory; however I believe that this
enables their interpretation to reflect more vividly their
artistic personality.

Here are some suggested methods for memorizing music
(these will usually be used in combination):

- Via structural analysis. The structure of a piece, once
  comprehended, can be conceived as a mental scaffold
  supporting the musical material as it successively
  unfolds.
- Through use of the voice. At first we sing it through
  silently whilst reading from the music; then progessively
  trying to do so without looking at it. We should next
  sing through it again as before, but this time out loud;
  this (rather than silently) will be found to be the more
  efficient way to learn. Moreover it will help us not only
  to learn how to phrase it in a more *cantabile* manner,
  but by our ear hearing it will afford the memory
  another means of grasping it. It is not necessary to
  vocalize, so long as we reproduce the relative rise and
  fall of the pitches. We may also conceive it as if it were a
  tune; *quasi* 'hearing' it as if from dictation we play it by
  ear as we would if we were singing to ourselves a tune
  that we already know. The traditional French method
  of *solfège* also uses the voice to serve a comparable
  didactic purpose. Initially sing only the rhythm, then
  the melody, progressively adding the articulation, and
  then the accentuation. Decide on the breath-spots, later
  writing them in the text.
- 'Visualizing' the text and 'reading' from it mentally.
  Copying it out in one's own handwriting will help it to
  'sink in'. Review individually the different parameters of
  pitch, rhythm, articulation, dynamic and accentuation.

- Practising it without reading from the text from as early a stage as possible, forcing oneself to negotiate any passages that are still unsure by relying on powers of deduction. It will be advisable to check the text periodically for accuracy (!).
- Repeatedly listening to a recording of it. While this will also impress it on the mind, we should guard against learning music 'parrot-fashion' – as if one were learning a written text without bothering to comprehend its meaning.

§4.11 Tone

Tone on the bassoon, or indeed on any wind instrument, is at least in part a matter of personal taste. What kind of bassoon tone-quality do we wish to produce? Like most of the sounds of the modern orchestra, the characteristic tone of our instrument has changed considerably over past years. This becomes evident not only if we listen to early recordings, or historic specimens being played, but also from a study of the way composers have orchestrated with it. Contemporary accounts can also give us some idea of how the instrument sounded to contemporary musicians down the ages. In Germany, the three to four key instrument that the Hamburg music critic Johann Mattheson had in 1713 called 'proud' (*stolz*) had by 1803 become for Heinrich Christoph Koch (Koch, 1803) 'the instrument of love', exemplified by the grateful role of an effortlessly projected tenor voice cast for it by Beethoven. That the sound retained a certain 'edge' or 'grain' is shown by the phenomenon of the so-called *Fagottzug* (bassoon stop), built into Austrian and South German fortepianos from ca1790 to 1835, which introduced a strip of parchment next to the vibrating string to produce a slight 'buzz'. In France the same held good, as shown by Pierre Cugnier's remark that bassoon tone should never be denuded of that kind of 'bite' (*mordant*) proper to it, giving it the necessary *timbre*, otherwise it would resemble the serpent (La Borde, 1780). In that country it was customary to quadruple it in the orchestra, doubtless to balance with its fellow woodwinds. At all periods there have undoubtedly existed contemporaneously regional variations in tone dictated by differences of instrument design and local taste.

Up to comparatively recently the French and the German models of instrument have been distributed fairly equally throughout the countries of the world. Each was perceived to have its characteristic and differing qualities of tone, which in 1961 were characterised by a well-known expert thus: "The normal tone of the French bassoon is thin, reedy, and rather nasal, and the different quality of tone between high, middle and low registers is marked. The normal tone of the German bassoon is full, round and even throughout." (Camden, 1961). There is now a tendency for these differences, both of type of instrument and of tone, to become ironed out and lost at the behest of international conductors and gramophone recording engineers. In the case of the oboe and clarinet, national fashions still vary – and indeed why not? It would indeed be sad if all instruments – and all orchestras for that matter – were ever to use identical types of instruments and start sounding the same.

How then might we define 'ideal tone'? We might argue that it is one which is not only beautiful in itself, but one which answers best to the demands of the greatest composers as they use it in the orchestra. It must balance well within the orchestration – i.e. project without forcing. This presupposes a sound with something of the oboe's capacity for penetration. If it is thinner rather than thicker in character, not only will this be better achieved, but it will be a readier vehicle for nuance and expression; thicker too often means inflexible and unvarying. The bassoon can never hope to equal the modern horn in roundness and weight of tone, so there seems little point in trying to compete with it in these respects. When bassoons and horns are used together, it is often a positive virtue for their respective differences of tone colour to be maximised rather than minimised. A thinner sound will be found easier to balance when, at the other extreme, *pianissimo* playing is required.

Regarding balance, it is ironic that the bassoonist in the orchestra will often be criticised by the conductor one moment for being inaudible in a solo passage, while in the next, for not being able to keep down enough. In classical times the cellos and basses were often doubled throughout by bassoons; Haydn reportedly once insisted in a letter on having bassoons to consolidate the bass line – not because they would be heard, but because if absent their presence would be missed. However they can sound obtrusive nowadays when both are left doubling in lightly scored passages.

How is the player to cope with these demands on his available range of tone? We can develop as large and free a tone as possible by trying to furnish ourselves with a set-up – instrument, crook and reed – which offers comparatively little resistance and will accept and respond to what we may choose to blow into it over as wide a range of response as possible. In this way only a minimum of expended effort is unproductive – i.e. used to overcome the basic resistance of the instrument. It will respond when we only give a little, and its response will be correspondingly greater when we give more. The instrument will not seem to be a constricting or limiting factor to what we are trying to put into it.

On our part we should accept the fact that the tone we produce is peculiar to us. However much we may try to model ourselves on a particular player that we admire, the actual tone that results is more likely to reflect the qualities inherent in us and our particular instrument rather than any imagined conception we may have. Our task should be to capitalize and exploit these qualities in order to produce as sonorous and beautiful a tone as possible. This we can best achieve by seeing that we are working as efficiently as possible to capitalize on our bodily resources – that we are using them to their best advantage. A fine tone is primarily conditioned by the breath. There must be a free flow of breath on which the tone can be floated. Good posture enables us to produce efficient breath support and an open throat and free neck and throat will ensure that the effort from below is not cancelled out by conflicting tensions elsewhere. We can improve the resonance of our tone by maximising the cavities inside the mouth, by keeping the jaw open, and by giving a firm support to the air column from the abdominal muscles.

We need to think of our instrument as a piece of acoustic apparatus which, when suitably excited, will sound and resonate. The degree to which it will resonate depends on the skill of the player. Far from imposing our demands on the instrument, we need to learn from it what kind of collaboration is required from us if we are to obtain the optimum signal from it. What scope do we have for acquiring a tone that is personal to us? If a fine actor is able to impersonate convincingly a variety of different roles, there should be scope for us to do justice to a wide range of different music by subtle modifications made through tone and style.

For a bassoon tone to be acceptable and pleasing today, it should possess the qualities of being 'dark', 'smooth', 'rich', 'full' etc. It should be free of extraneous noise factors, often caused by air escaping from the side of the mouth. The reed should deliver a sound that is comparatively free of 'reediness' and 'buzz', which were qualities associated with the French model bassoon in the earlier part of the 20th century when played indifferently. The sound should be centred and focussed, rather than diffuse – comparable to the signal of maximum intensity and amplitude of signal we obtain by careful tuning of the radio. It is such qualities that will help the sound to carry well and to penetrate the orchestral texture as required.

§4.12   Vibrato

1   Theory

Vibrato is widely employed on the bassoon nowadays as a valuable means of expression to embellish the tone. When judiciously used, it can either highlight individual notes or put those passages or phrases that warrant its use into higher relief. As an artistic effect it should be distinguished from mere tremulousness, which may be caused by lack of control, nerves, fatigue etc.

How long it has been used is hard to determine. A number of late 18th century authorities remarked on the notable resemblance of the bassoon to the human voice, which possibly indicates that some form of vibrato had been in use already at this time. According to a 19th century German authority: "The bassoon is serious, yet at the same time highly genial (*tief gemüthlich*). It is the man as he appears among his family, directing and arranging everything with absolute strictness, yet caring and tending as well with unswerving devotion." (Schilling, 1838), indicating a tone which, though often severe, was also capable of tender expressiveness. As early as 1832 the Russian Glinka marked *con vibrato* an expressive long solo passage for both clarinet and bassoon in the slow movement of his *Trio pathétique* – it is significant that he wrote it in a heightened emotional state whilst touring in Italy.

In historical times vibrato could be produced either by the finger or the breath. The former technique developed from the late 17th century first on flute and oboe (see Haynes, 2001), and consisted of making a trill-like movement of a free finger over an open tone hole so as to produce a fluctuation of pitch. Of necessity this was restricted to sustained notes within a phrase – and only certain notes at that. It was often notated with a wavy line placed over the note. Becoming obsolete during the 19th century, it was still being advocated on the bassoon in the tutors of Neukirchner (1840) and Jancourt (1847).

The use of breath vibrato on woodwind in the UK was pioneered by the oboist Leon Goossens, appointed to the New Queens Hall Orchestra in 1913. Up until quite recent times it was not customary for players of the German instrument to use it (see Philip, 1992) placing them at a disadvantage *vis à vis* players of the French instrument which, being more easily responsive to vibrato could, in the hands of a good player, outdo them in expressiveness. Gwydion Brooke's playing, first revealed in his ground-breaking recording of the Weber Concerto in 1947, ushered in a new concept of free vibrato and flexibility of phrasing. The reaction of Archie Camden was typical for its time: "There are various opinions regarding the use of vibrato. It seems to be generally agreed that a small amount of vibrato can give life, warmth, and vitality to the tone. I suggest that 'small' should be the operative word. The wide, throbbing kind of vibrato – wow-wow, wow-wow – is in bad taste, in my opinion, whether it is vocal or instrumental, and can easily make a bassoon sound like a badly played saxophone. [...] I asked the principal bassoonist of a famous continental orchestra his views on this subject. His answer was: 'Any player who uses vibrato in the classics should be shot.'" (Camden, 1961). This may be compared with: "le vibrato est mauvais et reservé aux amateurs" (Taffanel & Gaubert, 1923). Such attitudes seem strangely dated at the present time.

The distinguished flute player and teacher Marcel Moyse

took a fine baritone opera singer as his model for tone, style and vibrato (Moyse, 1971): as wind players, we can scarcely do better. When a singer's *melisma* momentarily lingers on a held note, a perceptible vibrato will ensue, a natural phenomenon which an instrumentalist will wish to copy. From the string player we might imitate certain idiosyncratic effects such as attacking a note 'cold' and then progressively warming the tone – although hardly the post-Kreisler mannerism of continuous vibrato throughout the duration of each and every phrase.

Let us try to stay within those aesthetic considerations which may be found generally acceptable today by disapproving of a vibrato:

- when it is used to bolster up and mask a tone lacking body and quality
- when it is used indiscriminately all the time both in solos and in the orchestra – even in woodwind passages of block harmony
- when it becomes a pitch wobble, either very fast or very slow.

It is by the judicious highlighting in this way of those elements of the phrase that are significant that will render it eloquent, rather than attempting to 'beautify' indiscriminately each and every note. Depending on the music in question, it might be employed only sparingly, or indeed not at all. But when it is be used, it should be applied audibly and with conviction – almost at times like a deliberate ornament. It should not be a mere blanket wobble over everything – like cream on a cake – but a varying and subtle means of highlighting the points of a phrase in order to heighten the expressiveness and eloquence of what we are playing. In ensemble music it will be found most pleasing when used to enhance the beauty of expression in solo passages – such as those in classical music marked *dolce*, and in other places where increased

The Bassoon

projection is called for. By its means, the sound is enlivened and enriched, so that the line of the phrase 'tells' more eloquently. There are many solo passages in the orchestral repertoire which, having heard a fine player employ vibrato to play them, would seem unthinkable without its judicious use: passages of Tschaikovsky and Ravel especially spring to mind here. Who would not wish to emulate the solo violinist in the Sibelius Concerto when entering after his cadenza? (Fig 53):

Fig 53
Reproduced by kind permission of Robert Lienau Musikverlag, Frankfurt am Main (Germany)

2 *Application*

How are we to achieve these effects? A vibrato can be produced on the bassoon in a number of different ways:

a   the player can shake the instrument causing the reed to oscillate between the lips

b   the player can move his head up and down causing the same reaction

c   moving the lower jaw up and down

d   causing the soft palate area of the throat to vibrate by creating a resistance there to blow against – this technique is experienced when we produce a vibrato whilst whistling

e   by a so-called 'diaphragm vibrato' technique, which is producing a series of nuances of intensity by causing

164

the steady support of the abdominal muscles (*rectus abdominalis*) to the air column to fluctuate with an even rhythmic pulsation

f by different combinations of these.

Let us take these alternatives in turn:

a unlike trumpet, our instrument is not one that it is practicable to shake whilst playing

b hardly conducive to maintaining the throat open; it also looks bad!

c affecting embouchure support by working with the jaw will tend to produce a fluctuation of pitch rather than of intensity (but note that this method is advocated for players of the French instrument (see Allard, 1975)).

d Using the throat does not allow for variation in speed and intensity. The conscious effort to produce a vibrato could also lead to a tightening and tensing of the throat and neck, which it is of prime importance to keep open and free whilst playing. It has been shown recently that the larynx may become involved during vibrato, but we should allow both larynx and throat to respond freely to the pulsations from below rather than deliberately initiate movements from there.

e That produced by the abdominal muscles is generally held to be the most efficient and satisfactory, allowing for speed and intensity to be controlled. This is the method that should be practised, although not until the player has sufficient mastery of basic playing technique. It should be pointed out that it is misleading to use the term 'diaphragm' for this kind of vibrato, implying that we are controlling it from the diaphragm (see p72). In fact it is not possible to exercise conscious control over the diaphragm. It is rather the muscles of the abdominal wall that are

165

The Bassoon

doing the job, from that part of the abdomen just above the pelvis in front up to the height of the navel extending around the flanks.

There is a certain paradox in the using of vibrato as a solo performer. To a certain extent the following decisions governing its use will be taken consciously at the moment:

- where (whether to a single note, or an entire phrase)
- at what intensity
- at what speed.

However its application later on will rather be instinctive, unconscious, possibly depending on how deeply our feelings are engaged. The task of our practice must be to school our muscles in vibrato technique – deploying varying degrees of intensity and speed over the entire compass – so as to make the technical resources available as and when required.

Ideally the use of vibrato should be controlled and deliberate in speed and intensity. As players of an eight-foot register instrument we do not need to vibrato at the speed of our higher-pitched colleagues. And just as the cellist will vibrate slower on the lower strings of his instrument than in the higher positions, so the speed of our vibrato will depend on the register we are playing in.

Because of varying resistance (for acoustic reasons associated with the pattern of tone-holes), certain notes will be more responsive and thus vibrate more freely than others. Such discrepancies must be allowed for. For vibrato to 'tell', the upper register will always require less effort on our part, the lower register more.

For a thorough treatment of the teaching of vibrato – indeed the first that is comprehensive – the reader is referred to Jooste's *The Technique of Bassoon Playing* (Jooste, 1984).

3 Routines

1   Isolate the different techniques listed below, so that by experiencing them we can recognize them if or when we use them:
- shake the instrument
- move the head up and down
- move the lower jaw up and down
- activate the throat (as in whistling)
- cause the support of the abdominal muscles to fluctuate
- use various differing combinations of the above methods.

2   From now on we will restrict ourselves to employing the abdominal muscles, with the object of teaching them patterns of use that they will be able to reproduce without our conscious control. Since basically the same muscles are employed, return to the earlier 'dog-panting' routines (§4.4, Routine 3, p77/8), using metronomic beats to practise regular pulsations gently at a precisely controlled tempo of ♩ = 30. At progressively enhanced speeds alternate firstly 'dog-panting' in-out with secondly playing (Fig 54):

Fig 54

§4.13   Practice (General Training)

Discussed here is the practising of technique in general, rather than of a specific piece of music – for which see the following section §4.14. All of these topics should be considered in the light of the principles set forth in §4.2.

1 Theory

How we progress as performers – our rate of improvement and our degree of achievement – will largely depend on the efficiency of our practice. It follows that it is worth devoting thought and care as to both how and what we practise.

In our practice we should aim to consolidate techniques that are sound, and to replace unsound techniques with sound techniques. Because man is a creature of habit, the constant repetition of a faulty technique will always tend to establish it. Therefore the substituted technique that corrects it must be even more frequently repeated if the old one is to be eradicated. It is heartening that the body, once it has experienced a new technique that it perceives to be more user-friendly, will tend to adopt it (even if we remain unaware of this process at the time).

The attitude we have to our instrument should be one of co-operation rather than of domination. We must view it with respect as a piece of acoustic apparatus that will resonate optimally according to how we excite it. Obtaining an extreme high note is like coaxing a genie out of his bottle, and only achieved when we supply what the instrument wants, and not what we think it ought to want. It is self-evident that the process of coming to terms with a strange instrument, or of blowing in a brand-new instrument, will require that the player learns how best to produce the effects he desires. Even when we have been using the same instrument for years there will always be something new that it can teach us.

We should try to practise with as generous a tone as possible so that we may develop a free and projecting sound. It will always be possible to give less, or dampen with the embouchure the excessive vibrating of the reed to produce less intensity if required. But if we habitually play in a restrained lack-lustre way, forcing of tone is more likely to ensue when we want more.

We should guard against the making of mistakes when we play. Thus our adopted practice speed should never exceed one thought likely to allow us to play without error. Repetition will tend to consolidate the faulty pattern, thereby making it more difficult to eradicate later on. Fingering mistakes must be analysed carefully when the manoeuvre has called for several fingers to move simultaneously, and particularly when both hands are involved. Only slow repetition of the manoeuvre will reveal the underlying cause.

Part of such non-specific practice should be devoted to the appraisal of how we are currently playing - something we might otherwise be too busy to consider. This could be compared with having a session of silent meditation in church, where we might be granted insights and ideas denied to us elsewhere. In this way we give ourselves a unique opportunity to re-assess our playing objectively. With the passage of time we ourselves alter, undergoing a continuous process of developing, maturing and aging; techniques that will have served us well earlier on may no longer retain their validity. Having identified those points of style / elements of technique that need correcting, we should devise and implement routines to replace bad patterns with good, wrong with right, less efficient with more efficient.

Whilst carrying out such procedures we should also take the chance to indulge in creative experimentation with techniques new to us - to try out alternative ways of doing something in order to verify which might work better for us. In this way useful insights may be gained. There are many techniques that we will learn better through the practical experiencing of them than by means of verbal or written description. Our best teacher will always remain our own self.

The amount of time, concentration and stamina available to us, being of necessity limited, is extremely precious. Therefore we must not squander it but aim for the maximum return per unit of time spent. Those who apparently practise least but are high achievers are probably those who have utilized their time with the maximum efficiency. Although the famous composer and pianist Dohnányi was reputed never to practise, his published sets of finger exercises are among the most ingeniously demanding of their kind. Nonetheless ample and sufficient practice time must be allotted, given the fact that most of us are slow to learn and to improve.

In our practice session, the order we choose to deal with different topics is important; we need to start off well, because patterns adopted at the outset will tend to persist. Crucial is the preliminary process of warming up. The athlete, about to run a race, needs to get on form before he can achieve optimum performance. If he warms up excessively, too much valuable energy will already have been spent; but if on the other hand he doesn't do enough, he will only get into his stride when it is too late. We who play are about to make heavy demands on our body; we cannot expect good collaboration until certain pre-requisites have been met. Each of us needs to learn what works best for the particular occasion.

A style of playing which is free from constricting tensions – a free and relaxed style – is desirable. This is more likely to be achieved if we intersperse those routines that are intense and tiring with those that are less taxing.

When we have achieved the finished result of playing well, we are carrying out many correct techniques simultaneously. It makes sense to identify these and practise each in isolation.

What makes the learning and teaching of breath-leading technique problematic is the fact that so much of the action is hidden and thus verifiable neither to ourselves nor to others. Matters are made even worse when we wear loose garments, since these will prevent anything from being seen; on the other hand if we wear little or no clothes and practise in front of a pair of mirrors, it is surprising how much it is possible to observe.

The systematic building up of strength, stamina and finger technique is more efficiently carried out by using practice routines rather than etudes. A methodical routine will cover a range of technical demands consistently and comprehensively in a way that no etude can ever match. The time thus saved from practising etudes is better devoted to art music.

In determining our practice priorities we might instinctively wish to concentrate merely on increasing the speed of finger and tongue. We should however bear in mind that, once we are reasonably competent, the most frequently occurring 'wrong-note' mistakes made when we play will be those caused by the non-speaking of notes on to which we have attempted to slur. The practice of scales in diatonic and chromatic intervals in *legato* will identify those intervals that require especial care and teach us how to cope with them.

2 Application

Environment
- The room acoustic should not be too flattering to avoid misconceptions regarding our quality of tone; we should on occasion play out in the open air in order to experience zero room-resonance.
- We should furnish ourselves with a chair that offers

what we require. It must support our lower back, if and when we need it to. The actual seat should preferably be hard rather than soft, raked forward rather than backwards, flat crosswise rather than dished, not so wide that it interferes with the instrument, and high enough for our legs to be vertical allowing our heels to rest on the floor. A height-adjustable stool with a firm upholstered seat, the rake of whose forward tilt is also adjustable, is ideal.

Equipment

- instrument: this should be in an adequate working-state
- reed: this should have a low threshold of resistance consistent with both general intonation and with response in the high register; aesthetic criteria need not always apply (the ideal reed should demonstrate an ability to sound at one extreme bottom A′, and top f″ at the other)
- metronome: electronic with visual indicator, rather than a mechanical type requiring a level base
- music-stand: adjusted to the right height
- mirror: ideally a pair positioned so that we can observe ourselves from both front and in profile (see Fig 3, p64)
- clock: to help us make optimal use of our limited time resources
- pencil, eraser and paper: for making notes.

Dress

Garments should not restrict mobility, hamper freedom, nor 'anaesthetize' sensation (see §4.4 *Faults / Problems* p84). Thus jeans and waist-belt that are too tight will prevent expansion of the lower abdomen, restricting breathing activity to the upper body. An over-tight belt can deaden in that part of the body the very awareness of sensation that we should strive to cultivate.

3 Routines

In a well-planned practice session each of the topics covered in the Routines of §4.4, §4.5, §4.6, §4.7, §4.8 and §4.12 should be touched upon, and adapted and abbreviated according to need and time available. It is recommended that they are dealt with in the order that follows:

1   *Breath – without Instrument*

- Dog-Panting: this establishes awareness of our abdominal muscles, getting them to work in isolation free of participation from elsewhere. We adopt a 'skiing' position in order to involve and activate the back muscles (Fig 9b, p77, Fig 10, p78).

- Reed Crowing: having got the abdominal muscles working, we next attend to achieving a favourable balance between their contribution and that of the embouchure. Take the reed, which to work must be moistened on both its outer and inner surfaces. The common method of doing this is to immerse it in a water-filled container kept in our case. An alternative method is as follows: rather than wetting it in water, take it dry. Having collected a quantity of saliva in the mouth, use the abdominal muscles to expel it with the utmost force through the blunt end in a short, sharp puff, so as to moisten the entire inner reed-surface; this will serve as a useful 'warm-up' routine in itself. Crow it, keeping count in units of five of the number of $\downarrow$ = 60 beats, trying conscientiously to sustain a 'triple-crow' for as long as possible – that is, not to give up until we have completely run out of air; keeping a tally over a sequence of three to five repetitions, we try to improve our score each time. We may have a conscious image of squeezing from below like a bagpiper pressing against the windbag with his elbow; however in so doing we should not allow the chest to sink, but maintain the chest in a state of non-interference (Fig 11, p79).

- Increase the demands by attempting to produce this crow with the crook attached.

2 *Breath – with Instrument*

- whether sitting or standing, carry out a check of basics of posture, of playing position
- long notes: C♯ *poco forte, tenuto, senza diminuendo* repeated in sequence, of maximum duration, timing in-breaths @ ♩ = 60 (Fig 14, p81).
- *sons filés*: according to requirement, sequences of either four or five notes, each of either dotted minim or semibreve in duration, striving for evenness of tone-quality (Fig 15, p81)
- to school control and increase available scope of dynamic: long tones in *crescendo* (Fig 16, p82), and *diminuendo* (Fig 19, p83)
- vibrato (Fig 54, p167)
- exercises foregoing embouchure (Fig 20, p84)

3 *Embouchure*

- reed on crook exercises to concentrate awareness of lip musculature (Fig 25, p102)
- promote flexibility and control (Fig 30, p106; 31, 32, p107)

4 *Tongue*

- routines for speed and stamina (Fig 42, p121)

5 *Fingers*

- trill routine (Fig 46, p133)
- tenor register scale routine (Fig 47, p133)
- selection from diatonic intervals scales routine (Fig 48a/b, p134/135)
- selection from chromatic intervals routine (Fig 49a/d, p136/139)
- chromatic scale
- selection from arpeggios routine (Fig 50, p140).

The perfect execution of a passage depends on an impeccable standard of finger, tongue and breath. Practise fingers alone without blowing, which enables us to concentrate on this aspect free of any other distraction. Hold the instrument in a position that allows them to be observed while they are at work. Then in playing position watch them in a mirror. Only when satisfied that the fingers can be relied on proceed to incorporate actual blowing.

4 Faults / Problems
We should guard against over-concentration on finger technique, leading to the neglect of such other important topics as control of dynamic and nuance.

§4.14   Preparation of new Material

See also §4.10 *Interpretation.*

1   Theory

When learning a piece of repertoire for the first time, there are basically two approaches open to us, both from the view-point of **Technique** and of **Interpretation**.

Technique
a   multiple run-throughs – at first slower, then progressively faster in the hope that, through constant repetition, the incidence of error will gradually lessen until a performance free of any mistake has been achieved
b   adopting a speed no faster than one commensurate with accuracy – however slow this may at first prove to be – with the object of avoiding mistakes at any cost; attempting the end-speed would thus be left until the very last.

The Bassoon

To **a:** considering that we are creatures of habit it might be argued that the constant repeating of mistakes – especially if their causes have not been ascertained and corrected – will tend to engrain the faulty patterns. We would be liable 'on the night' to revert to more familiar error-laden patterns, especially when there has been insufficient time for all trace of these to have been eradicated.

To **b:** called for here are qualities of:

- humility – in accepting that we are not as well-equipped with technique as we would wish to be
- patience – since the instilling of new skills through repetition sufficient for them to become engrained will require more time than we might wish or foresee
- self-confidence – daring to delay the adoption of the end-speed until we are 100% sure of ourselves, notwithstanding nervous pressures as the time of performance inexorably approaches; however we may confidently predict that the discharge of adrenalin on the night will see us through anyway (!).

Interpretation

a 'bash through' repeatedly in order to master the notes; only then, relying on what this may have taught us about the piece, starting to consider such supplementary matters as speed, phrasing, agogic, expression, interpretation etc.

b acquainting oneself as far as possible with the music before addressing the technical problems, in order to arrive at artistic decisions uninfluenced and unaffected by these.

To **a:** to attempt to prepare a work for performance that is new to us without first trying to get to know it musically is wasteful of time and can pose problems later on. We will hardly arrive at an optimum interpretation having played it through numerous times in a mechanical unmusical way.

To **b**: when preparing a new solo work (or indeed any ensemble-part) we need to remain constantly aware of the work as a whole and of the relationship that our individual part may bear to it. In the theatre, it would be unthinkable for an actor to learn his part whilst remaining unaware of the lines spoken by others on the stage. Thus in preparing a concerto, the role of the orchestral accompaniment must always be borne in mind. This is largely because the underlying harmony and configuration of the bass line will, to a large degree, prescribe and designate the phrasing and accentuation of the solo line. It is thus essential that in learning it the orchestral score is available for constant reference. In the case of a sonata with piano conceived as a duo for two equal partners (such as that by Hindemith), it is vital to be intimately acquainted with the piano part; this is hardly less true for duos of unequal partnership. Similarly, these must be prepared from the piano score, rather than merely the solo part on its own. The 18th century solo sonata was always printed in score anyway, with the figured bass below providing the soloist with the information essential for phrasing and embellishment; it is potentially disastrous that the average modern edition of such works, by printing the solo part on its own, fails to supply this vital information.

When we start work on a new piece, it is more efficient if we already have a yardstick by which to judge our interpretative efforts. Two examples illustrate this:

- When an orchestra rehearses a new work for the first time, it is only if the conductor already has a clear conception of how he wishes it to sound that he can make the most efficient use of the resources available – in this case the rehearsal time, and the improvement potential (and goodwill) of his players.

- The pianist Walter Gieseking, who was blessed with a phenomenal memory, has described how he prepared a piece of new repertoire. His first step was to sit in an armchair with the score and commit it to memory. While memorizing it, the basic decisions as to its interpretation would be considered and made. Only then would he commence his practice at the piano, his task now being the comparatively mechanical one of realizing in sound the artistic conception already in place (Gieseking & Leimer, 1972).

For these reasons stated I strongly advocate the second of the approaches outlined above – viz. **b** – regarding both **Technique** and **Interpretation**.

Performing a work for unaccompanied instrument poses special challenges. Here the soloist foregoes every support given by an accompaniment, such as helping the listener orientate himself as to matters of tonality and metre. It is instructive to listen to performances of works for other unaccompanied instruments in order to realize the problems that have to be overcome. In the case of a tonal piece, the opening bars must be played in such a way that the listener can orientate himself – enabling the time-signature to be grasped, the down-beat located, the tonality identified. It could be dangerous to indulge in too much *rubato* and agogic until we have allowed for this to happen.

2 *Application*

When addressing the task of learning a new piece of repertoire for the first time, the following procedures should be followed:

- Identify the main technical problems. Complexities of rhythm need to be tackled before those of pitch. Problems involving odd-number groupings of notes such as triplets, quintuplets, septuplets, etc. (especially when complicated by the addition of rests and syncopations) need to be clarified away from the instrument. Methods involving singing, clapping, playing on the keyboard, etc. may be found useful here; Hindemith's *Elementary Training for Musicians* gives many valuable routines of this sort (Hindemith, 1946).

- Determine which passages pose the worst problems for the fingers. Isolate such specific 'clusters' of rapid notes and write them out on manuscript paper, notating each note as a whole-note. Practise these by employing varying patterns of accentuation and rhythm. Some of the routines proposed below may be adapted here.

- Re-writing a passage enharmonically may sometimes facilitate comprehension of chromatic (or atonal) passages; it is sometimes worth re-writing obscure rhythmic groupings in simplified form.

- Any short passage offering particular problems should be memorized; this will help us in performance by aiding our concentration and guarding against distraction. It will also enable us to practise it with our eyes closed – a valuable aid to concentration.

The Marking of Parts

It must be emphasized that the marking of parts is an art, and one to be carried out with neatness and accuracy. If a concert has to be rehearsed a considerable time in advance, the decisions taken and insights gained need to be documented there and then. It is instructive to play from a part that bears multiple annotations added by former colleagues that warn of potential hazards, aid comprehension and thus prevent accidents. When a part has been played from over decades worldwide it is likely that every conceivable accident will already have occurred – and thus warned against.

The Bassoon

General

- Correcting of wrong notes; note that when an error has been identified it should be corrected permanently in ink, all earlier traces being removed with a knife. On the other hand, inauthentic *retouchements** asked for by the conductor should be added in pencil, identified as such, and afterwards erased (!).
- marking how the conductor beats (in 2, in 4 etc)
- where the beat starts to become subdivided
- *rit., rall.*: indicated by a wavy line above the system
- indicating, where warranted, where the beats fall within the bar: indicated above the relevant notes or rests by vertical dashes (Fig 55a) or brackets (Fig 55b):

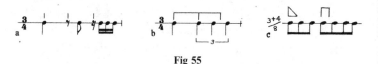

Fig 55

- identifying a note or phrase that is significant and/or exposed – either by a simple inverted 'tick' written above ⌃ρ, by drawing 'spectacles' ♂°, or writing *Solo* above
- the provision of cues
- the subdividing of lengthy periods of bars rest into recognizable units
- indicating the subdivision of quintuplets (3 + 2, or 2 + 3) and septuplet (3 + 4, or 4 + 3) by 'triangle' / 'house' symbols (Fig 55c)
- in a principal part, adverting entries by the Second, Third or Contra player.

Bassoon-specific

- Identify any slurs that might be potentially risky: annotate those that merely require care with a simple

---

* a term used for interventions to the music text

180

bracket; those that require remedial treatment to enable them to 'speak' – such as the use of supplementary keys – would be marked differently

- If – exceptionally – it is deemed necessary to employ a special fingering rather than a standard one, this may be indicated below the note in question by means of a diagram. This will be necessary in the case of such special effects as multiphonics etc
- where the crook-lock needs to be applied, or removed: special symbols may be used
- instructions for of double tonguing by writing *tk tk* above the relevant notes, for triple tonguing *tkt ktk, tkt tkt*, or *ttk ttk*
- breath-spots should on occasion be decided upon and notated in the part (note that if a comma were to be used, this might be confused with a caesura)

A breathing mark acts in two ways: both as a positive instruction and as a mandatory warning not to breathe elsewhere. Breath-spots should be carefully chosen with sensitivity to the overall phrasing and structure of the music. A supplementary breath taken early on will sometimes be required to tide one over a long successive passage. An intake of breath, taken independent of physical requirements, can often be used to heighten the expressiveness of a phrase, as in Pierné's *Solo de concert* (Fig 56):

Fig 56

The Bassoon

Marks by the composer indicating articulation and phrasing should be scrupulously observed and made audible. In the following passage (Brahms *2nd Piano Concerto* op.83 iii) the melody is first announced by solo cello, and then repeated by 1st violins and bassoon. Each time the composer specifies an articulation in pairs of notes, but phrased at first in bar units. We should not be seduced by string players into ignoring this (Fig 57):

Fig 57

When determining in the orchestra the phrasing of a melody, we need to consider our solo line with relation to the underlying harmony and its accompaniment. This, together with resolving problems of co-ordination and balance, will require us to have access to the score and to consult it.

3 Routines

1   Identify those specific passages – sequences of up to a dozen-odd notes – that present especial difficulty, in order to work at these on their own. If possessing keyboard skills it is a good idea to play them on the piano so as to familiarize our ear with the pitches involved; using all ten fingers most passages will be comparatively easy to play. If the problem is in part rhythmic, we should sing it whilst simultaneously beating time. Start slowly at first, then progressively increase the speed. If there are comparatively short passages that challenge the fingers, the following routines for practising may be adopted:

182

- having written out the passage in white notes, use this as a basis for practising *sempre legato* in various rhythmic permutations – dotted rhythms, *syncopes* (syncopated figures), triplets etc
- 'picking fingers', or interspersing open 'f' (with all fingers removed from tone-holes and keys) between each note – i.e. interrupting a sequence of fingerings by reverting to 'all off' after each; this will draw individual attention to each fingering in turn
- taking a difficult sequence of (e.g.) a dozen notes and having supplied each with a number, practise each pair of notes as an interval tremolo accented first in duplets (*ab, ab, ab, ab*, then *ba, ba, ba, ba*), then in triplets (*aba, bab, aba, bab*) (a) merely fingered in silence and (b) then blown.

2 Given that the finished result will require that a number of different routines be carried out error-free and simultaneously, we need in our practice to identify and isolate successively the different parameters of pitch, rhythm, articulation, accentuation and dynamic. Before addressing the problem of the notes themselves, we should initially sing out loud in a monotone the rhythm, while beating time with a finger; then progressively add the marks of

- articulation
- accentuation
- dynamic.

Having decided on the breath-spots we may now take the instrument and practise the notes themselves. Once these are mastered, we may then proceed gradually to incorporate the marks. A passage from Berg's *Violin Concerto* will serve to illustrate this process (Fig 58):

The Bassoon

Fig 58
© Copyright 1936, 1996 by Universal Edition A.G., Wien / ph 537, UE 10903

§4.15   Performing Solos

Preparation

- when making travel plans, allow enough time for self, instrument and reeds to acclimatize, especially in extremes of climate or altitude
- allow time for the work done during the practice sessions to be absorbed and consolidated well in advance of the actual performance
- if we intend to play from memory we should do so from an early stage; consult frequently with the score for verification purposes
- at the end of each practice session, give a performance run-through without stops, so that the current standard can be objectively assessed
- play through the entire programme daily over preceding days
- set up one or more semi-formal occasions just before the concert where the programme is performed before invited friends
- when rehearsing an orchestral concerto with piano, ensure that the accompanist plays from a reduction that

faithfully reproduces the orchestral score; insist that the dynamic markings are observed as far as possible.

Concerto Preliminaries

- arrange to consult the conductor in advance, having prepared a list of points to discuss; try to forestall eventual problems of balance
- check orchestral material for anything that might waste valuable rehearsal time – e.g. appoggiaturas written out wrongly in the Mozart Concerto K191, and (more mundanely) missing bar numbers or rehearsal letters, dynamics, solo cues, tempo changes and so forth; best of all, use one's own material.

Recital Preliminaries

- ascertain pitch of piano and suitability of chair if required
- try to guarantee an adequate level of general fitness and of sleep.

On the Day

- Determine the optimum geographical position for bassoonist and pianist to adopt on stage. While being sited to the right of the pianist in front of the well of the piano is good for mutual visibility, this can mean that the bassoon is absorbed by the piano sound. Tonal separation is better if the bassoon is on the left in front of the pianist. Note that having the piano lid open on a short stick can focus its tone and make it louder than when fully open. Face the audience obliquely so that the bassoon is aligned parallel to the front of stage. Find a position for the music-stand so that it does not create an obstacle between artist and audience.

The Bassoon

- if bedroom facilities are available, spend one hour (or less) before the concert by taking a hot shower, spending 30-40′ in bed, taking a cold shower to wake up, then dressing
- stimulate the blood circulation to hands by filling adjacent wash-hand-basins with very hot and cold water and immersing the hands successively in each
- adopt a personal band-room routine which might include, after a brief warm-up (see §4.13), relaxing by lying on the floor, with head on a book and knees up (see Fig 8a, p76).

On Stage

- verify tuning in advance so as to be able to start promptly without preluding; if necessary, ask pianist to identify the key of the piece (if tonal) with an unobtrusive chord – since there is little point in being given an 'A' (!)
- try to establish eye-contact with members of the audience
- if fitting, do not forego the opportunity to address the audience by way of a few introductory words – this 'breaks the ice' for both audience and performer.

§4.16   Ensemble / Orchestral Skills

Most of such skills can only be acquired through practical experience rather than learned from reading a book. The best way to train is through observing and working with colleagues more experienced than we. If we are lucky, they will have the forbearance to point out to us our mistakes – especially those of which we are unaware – and help us correct them.

While the inexperienced car-driver spares little attention for his driving mirror or side mirrors, as confidence and experience is gained he will devote most of his attention to other road-users. Likewise, the player must learn to devote his main attention to his colleagues and the conductor rather than to his own problems. Synchronisation, intonation and balance are all-important.

Good ensemble players are like team-footballers – always ready for the ball, and ready to pass it on to the right colleague.

Small Ensemble

Performing chamber-music is satisfying in many ways. There is the feeling of enhanced artistic responsability, without conductor as intermediary. Especially rewarding can be the feeling of interdependence where if one were suddenly to take extra freedom over a solo phrase one's colleagues would instantly respond. When a work is constantly repeated on tour it can happen that the interpretation becomes progressively more free and idiomatic – coming to reflect more vividly the musical personality of the group. Without need for discussion, those ideas that have proved effective will be implemented in the future whilst those that don't work will simply be discarded.

Playing in a Wind Quintet poses special problems of balance, given the diversity between the instruments and according to how each is being used. The bassoonist is constantly discharging different functions and has to judge the balance accordingly without a conductor to guide him. When rehearsing new repertoire, it is almost obligatory to have a score available that all can consult easily – otherwise a massive wastage of time will ensue. Decisions arrived at in rehearsal must be documented by intelligible annotations to the part (see §4.14); this is especially important

The Bassoon

when there is a lapse of time between rehearsal and performance. Marks entered might include:

- the correcting of misprints, mistakes
- the adding of cues
- indication of solos
- indication of where to lead (especially at changes of tempo)
- identifying the instrument with the leading voice, to aid balance
- identifying danger spots and accident-prone passages
- markings to aid comprehension of complex time-signatures and rhythmic groupings.

Orchestra

In the orchestra the bassoonist also needs to be aware of the nature of his role in the music as it constantly changes – whether subordinate, secondary or primary. To achieve a satisfactory balance, he needs to be constantly listening and weighing up the situation.

The role of Second Bassoonist can often pose a greater challenge than that of First; as such we may at any moment be required to discharge the functions of

- inner voice, where needed to play softer than the First
- of bass to the wind section, where needed to play louder than the First
- of soloist, where needed to play as loudly as the First
- having to ignore the printed dynamic in order to balance correctly – room acoustic also needing to be taken into consideration.

Regarding intonation, we have to be flexible in our ability to respond and adjust as necessary. Given the relative infrequency of exposed solos, these are more challenging when they do occur.

A correct working relationship between Principal, Second and Contra is crucial, each having his own particular and identifiable role to play. Given the stress that can attend concerts and recording sessions, there needs to be a good-humoured atmosphere of mutual respect which, making due allowance for accidents and 'off-days', will also allow for constructive criticism all round. As individuals and as a section, our responsabilities are to the music, the organisation (if permanent members of an orchestra), and to the conductor – in that order(!).

§4.17 Exam, Competition, Audition

Each of these poses a challenge for our resources of nerve and courage to confront and overcome. As such they will usually prove in the long run to have been valuable and instructive. The following hints derive from experience gained 'on both sides of the fence'.

1 Exam

- Preparation: we should ensure that adequate time has been allotted beforehand for preparation (see below).
- Repertory: we should, if we can, choose something we like and enjoy playing, then learning it will prove more enjoyable. It should demonstrate what we are good at – rather than reveal potential weaknesses. We need to assess objectively what our strong points are so that we can choose these to display in the shop-window.
- Scales: before commencing, take whatever time is needed to reflect and pre-programme brain and fingers. Adopt slow speeds for the sake of safety. Once having

started, keep going ruthlessly, resisting any temptation to stop.
- Mistakes: we should brazenly ignore any accident that might occur, in order to minimize any possible knock-on effect.

2   Competition

There has been a proliferation of national and international competions in recent times, attributable to various factors. As prizes are now seen as an indispensable entrée to a solo career, concert managers and impresarios can thus avoid having to make value-judgments for themselves. This development must be seen as undesireable for various reasons, not least because jury decisions are often perceived in retrospect to have been wrong-headed.

Risks

- the inevitable lack of concensus among jurymen concerning matters of tone, style, interpretation etc.
- juries unduly affected by the 'Beckmesser-syndrome' (the detection of wrong notes), sheer accuracy being the only topic that can be objectively assessed and agreed upon
- opting for safety and accuracy in preference to the inspirational taking of risks
- undue nationalistic bias displayed by the jury: where the 'host' nationality predominates amongst jury and candidates, foreigners might be at a disadvantage
- among those jurymen that are also teachers, 'horse-trading' where their own students are concerned
- differences in the rules governing the awarding of marks and jury decision-making may lead to varying standards of fairness

- when the pitch of the accompanying piano – whether 440Hz, 442Hz or 444Hz – has not been divulged in advance, some competitors will be placed at a disadvantage
- with regard to bassoon, the whole question of *Fagott* vs *basson* introduces a complicating factor.

Benefits

- we are motivated to practise more than otherwise and thus improve our standard of playing
- we will often learn useful stimulating new repertory
- we might be forced to play from memory some of the time
- we will listen to and learn from our fellow competitors; we are being offered the opportunity of comparing our standards against an international yardstick
- we will meet and socialize with our international peer group, which may lead to valuable personal and professional contacts in the future
- we can make potentially useful contact with jurors
- we will gain the experience necessary for doing better next time
- we will learn by experience how to cope with 'nerves'
- we will have the satisfaction afterwards, whatever the result, of having achieved something worthwhile.

Hints

- note that those employing their own accompanist will always be at a distinct advantage over those that have to make do with the 'house' pianist
- prepare the programme as far as possible from memory
- allot adequate time in advance for the entire process of preparation
- set up occasions to perform the programmes under

quasi test conditions; try to visualize conditions on the day in advance
- allow sufficient time after arrival to acclimatize and prepare
- prepare psychologically as far as possible by trying not to set too great importance on winning
- listen to as many of the other candidates as possible, especially to the prize-winners.

3 *Audition*

Note that much of the foregoing may also be applied here. Appointment to an orchestral post via competitive audition, rather than by nomination, is increasingly the rule these days, especially as more qualified players compete for fewer work-openings.

- experience is necessary for learning the techniques needed in order to be successful
- discover as much as possible about the prospective job, especially the pitch employed
- consider the 'identi-kit' of whom is being sought, so that tone and style can be modelled accordingly; different qualities will be looked for, according to the type of post to be filled
- attend to smartness of dress and deportment
- trying to feel nonchalant – trying not to want the job too much – can often pay off psychologically.

Orchestral Passages
- prepare from the full score (preferably) or from the part, rather than from any other source: beware of published albums, which are often full of inaccuracies
- ensure acquaintance with the tempo, musical style and accompaniment; if necessary use recordings to work with

- scrupulously observe every dynamic, every nuance, the length of each note, maintaining good rhythm without recourse to foot-tapping; allow for adrenalin to affect perception of speed
- prepare the more important passages from memory
- assemble your own anthology, best self-copied by hand.

Preparation
- try to ensure being fit by adopting a regime of sufficient sleep and suitable diet; take up some compensatory sporting activity as well
- work to a planned practice-schedule, with a count-down by the week, by the day
- strive to dispense with the 'crib': i.e. by relying on memory as far as possible; at the very least, memorize concerto cadenzas and 'lead-ins'
- try to visualize the actual circumstances on the day, e.g. whether in an empty hall, or behind a screen
- be prepared to have to sit down to play
- perform mock run-throughs, ideally also before an audience in a hall
- allow adequate journey-time for acclimatization of reeds and instrument on arrival, to overcome jet-lag and journey fatigue.

§4.18   Teaching

General

All bassoonists should take an intelligent interest in the teaching process. Those who, for whatever reason, fail to make it as full-time professionals will find themselves having to teach for their livelihood, while those who are successful as performers will in due time be asked to accept pupils anyway.

The Bassoon

The student needs guidance not only on what he or she is to practise, but on how to go about it. In order to check on the procedures adopted, practice should be carried out under scrutiny in the lesson.

Lessons should judiciously include the consideration of both technical and musical matters.

Students should be accompanied on piano as often as possible so that they can experience and learn their music in its wider harmonic context.

Young Beginner
At what age is it best to start? This might depend on a number of factors. It can be objectively shown that an early start on bassoon is by no means as vital as in the case of other instruments; Klaus Thunemann, one of today's most distinguished virtuosos, did not start until 19 – having trained until then as a pianist. Previous experience on one or more other musical instruments is indeed beneficial – piano plus another woodwind would be ideal. Most important of all is to have had some singing experience – at however modest a level.*

As in any kind of instruction, it is the very earliest stages that are most crucial for the laying of a sound foundation for later progress. The teacher needs to make sure that the most fundamental principles are dealt with first, that they are grasped and correctly put into practice right from the very beginning.

- Adopting a favourable playing position poses a challenge to the young student for whom the instrument can be relatively large and heavy; the support-systems will

* An instrument designed for children pitched a 4th or 5th higher, with basic key-system and using standard-size reed, was developed in the mid 1990s by Guntram Wolf, Kronach, and successfully introduced into the UK as the 'mini-bassoon' by Howarth, London. Wolf had revived the earlier practice of making such instruments already in 1992 by building a tenor bassoon for the English player Richard Moore.

need choosing with care; 'short-reach' key-systems can help those with small hands; the shape of crook needs also to be considered

- processes such as tonguing that cannot be checked visually must be described verbally
- explanation needs to be frequently supplemented by practical demonstration; the traditional duet for pupil and teacher can hardly be improved upon
- since there are some techniques that are best learned by experiencing them oneself – rather than hearing them explained – the teacher needs to devise mechanisms that enable the student to teach himself
- the student should from time to time be accompanied on piano so that he can learn the piece in its wider context
- every student needs guidance on how to practise; this requires carrying out under scrutiny in the lesson
- the lesson should cover both technical and musical considerations
- reeds should be obtained from the teacher, rather than the student be required at too early a stage to make them himself; while needing to be balanced, they should offer enough resistance to help the student develop the necessary strength and support
- entering for grade exams can be a motivating factor and should ideally offer a yardstick for the standard achieved
- playing in school orchestras and other *ad hoc* groups, and participation in local competitive festivals should be encouraged.

Mature Amateur

- the student's motivation to study will be in order to enhance the pleasure he derives from music-making – be it amateur orchestra or chamber group; his course of study should be designed accordingly

The Bassoon

- objectives set should be realistic and capable of being achieved in the relatively short term
- encouragement should be freely offered; the teacher's success will be measured by the regularity with which lessons are requested (!).

Conservatoire Entrant

- it is the passing of the entrance exam that is at issue; among those topics to which time should be devoted are sight-reading skills and how to give a good interview
- experience with grade exams (Associated Board etc) will prove useful, as also will having participated in local festivals and youth orchestra courses
- lessons should be regular and of sufficient duration
- the piece(s) offered should be chosen with care and rehearsed thoroughly with an accompanist in advance.

Conservatoire Student

Let us first consider the conservatoire teacher from the student's perspective. Depending on the institution employing them, they fall into two categories: those who as part-timers combine teaching with outside professional work, and those that teach full-time.

The part-timer will usually also occupy a position in the local orchestra or opera house. Immediate day-to-day contact with professional music-making – giving great performances of great works – can stimulate the teaching and render it topical and practical (the student can even at times be offered practical involvement). On the other hand the inevitable clash of touring engagements can interrupt the rhythm of lessons; the higher the profile of outside career, the higher the rate of absence. Worse still, the appointment may have been made on reputation as performer rather than on proven pedagogical skills.

196

The other kind of conservatoire teacher will usually enjoy the status of university professor. The selection method will accordingly be more rigorous, being designed to guarantee professional and dedicated teaching of the highest calibre. Before being appointed the candidate will have given a lesson, one each to a junior and senior student before a peer-group panel of professors, and have performed a public recital. Once appointed they will be expected to relinquish any outside orchestral post held; but in some cases they may never have had any practical experience of this sort anyway(!).

Thus the teacher of either category may offer differing advantages – or disadvantages – to the student.

- Reeds: instruction should be given on not only on how to play the instrument but also how to cope with reeds i.e. how to adjust ready-made reeds, how to make them both from pre-formed stages and (later on) relatively from scratch. However it should be pointed out that violin students are not asked to adjust a sound-post or re-hair a bow, tasks undertaken by the professional luthier; reed-making, while enjoyable for the gifted few, should not monopolize time needed for other tasks - especially for juniors.
- in planning the curriculum, a judicious balance should be struck between technical and artistic material; time spent on etudes should not exceed that spent on art-music.
- The student should be guided in his choice of repertory over the course of his studies. It should be as comprehensive as possible, covering from the 17th century to today, avoiding transcriptions where possible; 'study-concertos' by lesser composers (see §6.2) should be learned before addressing mainstream repertoire (Mozart, Weber); the same applies to the 'salon duo', saving Saint-Saëns and Hindemith until less sophisticated works have been tackled.

- the student should obtain and use his own music rather than rely on borrowed material; such copies bearing his own markings will form a resource invaluable for use later on
- performing regularly in chamber-music and recital should form part of the curriculum
- the student should be encouraged to take down notes after each lesson; the teacher also needs to maintain his own written records
- students benefit if the teacher intersperses one-to-one lessons with class tuition
- students should always be allowed to accept occasional offers of professional work outside
- the student should be encouraged to participate in and to audit master-classes given by outside tutors and to enter for competitions, especially those held abroad.

Giving a Master-class

- these are more stimulating if, as an outsider, we can objectively present a differing and mildly controversial viewpoint
- it is the audience, as much as the individual student, to which the ideas should be presented
- generous allowance should be made for nerves
- depending on the time allotted, no more than one specific topic per student should be addressed
- we should try to address those areas where instant improvement can most likely be effected.

Five
Repertory & Use

§5.1 General

Orchestral Music

The role played by the bassoon in the orchestra has essentially changed over the course of the centuries. In the earliest period it was used to consolidate the bass line, forming part of the *continuo* group of instruments. By the time of J. S. Bach it formed the natural bass to the woodwind group – see such works as his Orchestral Suites I and IV. In France such composers as Rameau often assigned it an independent inner part, using it in a higher tessitura than was then current in Germany. J.C. Bach, benefiting from the talented playing of Felix Rheiner in Mannheim, allotted the bassoon a more soloistic role in several of his operas. The young Mozart, while employing the available pair of bassoons to double the bass line, increasingly used it in a more solo capacity – first as a pair, then forming part of a small obligato group. By the time of Beethoven the bassoon had extended its capability beyond that of the bass-register member of the wind group; it could now as a tenor voice vie with clarinet and oboe in matters of artistic expression. Joseph Haydn had been among the first to capitalize on its other qualities – its capacity for wit and humour, its unique character in staccato, its agility over a wide range and its plaintive high register. While Mendelssohn exploited its capacity for humour in *A Mid-*

summernight's Dream, Weber assigned it a more dramatic role in *Der Freischütz*. By the early 19th century in France Berlioz felt the necessity of scoring for two pairs in the orchestra; this was followed in Italy by late-period Verdi. In Germany Wagner had from ca 1850 started to employ three (to be copied later by Strauss and Mahler), though it was not found necessary elsewhere to enlarge the section. In Russia composers could confidently demand the widest range of expression and technique – such as Tschaikovsky in his symphonies and Rimsky Korsakov in *Sheherazade*. The spectacular development in woodwind manufacture and performance in Paris from the 1880s had its effect on the works of composers exposed to it – whether natives like Debussy and Ravel, or foreigners such as Stravinsky, whose orchestral solos for the *basson* of their time are notable.

Chamber Music

The pre-Baroque repertory includes works for violin, *fagotto* and continuo by Marini, Fontana and others. The Baroque repertory includes notable trio sonatas by Vivaldi, Handel and Zelenka. The earliest role of the bassoon in Classical period chamber music was as supporting bass instrument to the standard *Harmonie* grouping of pairs of oboes – and / or clarinets – and horns. There was a vogue among the aristocratic courts of central Europe for wind arrangements of popular music – Vienna alone boasting over 100 such professional groups – and quantities of original music for these forces came to be written. Mozart supplied a large corpus of such *Harmoniemusik* scored for wind groups ranging from sextet, octet to as many as thirteen players in his *Gran Partita* K361. Notable contributions to this genre were also made by Haydn, Beethoven and Krommer. Mozart's genial idea of combining four winds with keyboard resulted in 1783 in one of his greatest works (K452), written for the bassoonist Ritter (Pl 14, next page), which was later emulated in 1796 by Beethoven (op 16). The wind quintet as ensemble group was first patronized in Paris by Reicha in the 1810s and soon adopted elsewhere by Danzi and others. Beethoven's successful idea of grouping strings with winds in his Septet of 1799 was copied by Schubert in his Octet of 1828.

After a comparative lull, the 20th century has seen a remarkable resurgence of wind chamber music. Concert activity in Paris caused many composers there to write for woodwinds; the reed trio became a favoured medium to which Villa-Lobos, Ibert, Milhaud and Françaix made notable contributions. Poulenc's sympathetic writing for bassoon in his duo, trio and sextet makes the loss of the sonata – unfinished at his death – the greater. While the outstanding modern wind quintet is that of Nielsen, contributions by Hindemith, Schoenberg, Barber and Françaix (to name just a few) are also notable.

Solo Repertory

The bassoon possesses less solo repertory than the other woodwinds – in terms of both quantity and quality. When considering the question of why this should be, it is worth reminding ourselves that composers seldom write unless for a specific reason. Most of those commissioning music for bassoon have been aristocrats or wealthy individuals attracted to the instrument (often amateur bassoonists themselves); their identity is often revealed on the relevant title-page. From among these categories of 'onlie begetter' we may salute the following individuals:

- Duke Friedrich Franz I, Duke of Mecklenburg-Schwerin (1785-1835), of whom it was alleged in 1826

Plate 14
Bassoon virtuoso Georg Wenzel Ritter (*b* Mannheim 1749, *d* Berlin 1808),
fl. Mannheim, Paris, Munich and Berlin; soloist (incl. tours 1774 to London and
Dublin), teacher (over 60 students, incl. Ozi and Brandt) and composer
(concertos, quartets). He premiered K297b and K452 for Mozart, who alluded to
him (letter of 18 vii 1778) as *der brave Holzbeißer* (the good wood-biter).
Reproduced by courtesy of the National Library, Vienna

that bassoon was his *Lieblingsinstrument* (favourite instrument); the wealth of bassoon music that survives in his library testifies to this

- King Max of Bavaria (1756–1825), who in 1811 agreed to commission Weber to write a concerto for his Court bassoonist Friedrich Brandt
- Baron Thaddäus von Dürnitz (1756–1807), in 1775 Mozart's Munich patron, an amateur player and composer for his instrument
- Jacques Hartmann (1774–1839), the wealthy proprietor of a textile factory in Munster, Alsace (still in business to this day) and accomplished amateur bassoonist for whom Brandl, Danzi and Gebauer composed solo works in the 1820s.

Otherwise it has been a case of virtuosos writing for their own use – as their public would then have demanded of them; among the more prolific were Ozi, Gebauer, Jacobi and Jancourt. The answer to our question is that, by comparison with other instruments, the bassoon is under-represented statistically in every one of the above categories.

On occasion a work for bassoon is written as part of a canon of works intended for an entire family of instruments, as in the case of Telemann, Saint-Saëns and Hindemith.

Solos with Keyboard

The nine sonatas by Bertoli (1645) constitute the earliest set of any sonatas for solo instrument with figured bass. These, together with comparable works by Selma and Böddecker, demand a remarkable degree of virtuosity. The extreme key of Telemann's sonata features what was evidently for the composer – himself a double-reed player – the *triste* character of the early 18th century instrument; others by Fasch and Schaffrath in Germany and Galliard and Merci in England reflect a more cheerful spirit. In France the large number of duets published by such composers as Boismortier and Corrette – much of it alternatively for gamba or cello – testifies to a lively market for such music. It is arguable that many such apparent duos are sonatas with unfigured keyboard accompaniment in disguise; as well as the outstanding Sonata K292 by Mozart there are similar sets by Devienne, Gebauer and Pleyel. In a class of its own is the highly original Sonata of 1807 by Anton Liste, a large-scale duo for two equal protagonists unequalled hitherto in the wind repertory. The 100-odd solo works written later in the 19th century by the Paris virtuoso Jancourt remain a unique and under-valued oeuvre. Of 20th century works, those by Hurlstone, Longo, Saint-Saëns, Hindemith, Castelnuovo-Tedesco and Tansman are outstanding. Greatest of all is the monumental *Sonata Concertante* of 1943 by Skalkottas.

Solos with Orchestra

Any discussion of the bassoon concerto has to start with the remarkable set of 39 works by Vivaldi that survive in score in Turin. But it is a sad fact that far too little is known of the circumstances of their composition, even for the instrument for which they were intended – whether for dulcian or bassoon – an area deserving of future research. Although concertos by such composers as Boyce, Haydn and Leopold Mozart have failed to survive, there exist in surprising quantity others by lesser masters. In Germany modest examples by Graun, Graupner, Fasch and Müthel were followed by a pair by J.C. Bach. England produced examples published by the amateur Hargrave and the organist Bond. The outstanding concerto of the bassoonist's repertoire remains that of Mozart. Although the least mature of any concert work of his in the repertoire, it remains an astonishing achievement by the 18 year-old composer; sadly we know nothing about the circumstances of its composition. Hummel's concerto, substantial though somewhat conventional, may be seen as its not unworthy successor. In France at this time the bassoon concerto became especially popular due largely to such composer-virtuosos as Ozi, Devienne and Gebauer. In Bohemia a repertory of 60/70 concertos between 1720 and 1830 by such composers as Kozeluch, Stamitz and Fiala survive. In Central Europe Danzi, Jacobi, Kalliwoda and David left attractive concert works. In a class of their own are the concerto and *Andante & Rondo Ungarese* written by Weber in his early twenties; together they form an outstanding pair of concert solos that epitomize the essential features of the instrument. In Italy a candidate for Rossini's lost concerto has recently surfaced, as has a manuscript by the youthful Verdi. In the 20th century there are notable works by Pierné, Elgar, Villa-Lobos, Jacob, Jolivet, Gubaydulina and Françaix. While Nielsen's planned concerto sadly never materialized there are late *concertante* works by Strauss and Hindemith.

Solos – Chamber Music

The pioneering set of quartets for bassoon and string trio by Ritter (Pl 11) were soon followed by a surprising quantity of such works by Carl Stamitz, Danzi, Reicha and others, well over a hundred of which survive. From the mid 1790s onwards a remarkable set of bassoon works was produced by Brandl, including three quintets with strings and three quintets with piano and string trio (a combination unique to him). In our time there have been notable works by Françaix and Jacob.

205

§5.2.1 Performance Notes on the Mozart Bassoon Concerto K191 (186e)

It is not proposed here to give suggestions regarding every point of phrasing and articulation – but rather to offer general guidelines on performance. Although Mozart's manuscript is no longer available to us today, it was until the early part of the 19th century in the possession of its original publisher J.A. André. It was dated, as far as we know, either 4th or 5th June 1774. The 'urtext' edition by Franz Giegling for the *Neue Mozart Ausgabe* (*NMA*, New Mozart Edition) for Bärenreiter, reprinted as Bärenreiter Study Score ♯253 (1981) has superseded all of the earlier editions, and should now be used in preference to any other. Note that the Breitkopf & Härtel orchestral material contains certain errors and requires correcting in a number of spots.

bar
I. Allegro

1-34	it is advisable to play in the opening *ritornello*; by doing thus the tempo can be established and both player and instrument warmed up, while the *tutti* sound benefits from the added colour
35,36	accentuation as in V1 in bar 1, i.e. with the main accent falling on the down beat – played with a down-bow – rather than the emphasis being given to the syncopated minim
37	the reiterated e♭'s with *crescendo*
38	trill to commence on upper note, without *Nachschlag*,* slurring to d' (matching V1), with *diminuendo*

---

* Nachschlag: turn at the end of a trill

39	the d′ to sound like an appoggiatura, i.e. accented, timed as 'triplet-syncope'
40	the bb on the down-beat belongs to the preceding phrase, which is repeated at the end of this in slightly varied form; thus the scale f to f′ connecting these two phrases may appear as in parenthesis
35-42	this opening gambit is of two components: after the 'hunting-call motif' opening, the melodic response is in contrast
45	the relationship of the two f′s is comparable to that of the two bbs in 35
47	the c′ downbeat is the culmination of the preceding rising arpeggio figure; the static lingering on b♮ enables the interest to transfer to the trill-figure on V2 and Va (note that this trill, restored by *NMA*, is missing in both the *GA* and the Breitkopf material)
48	C belongs neither to the preceding phrase nor to that which follows; it is better to take a breath before g′
50	as in 38
51-54	to be accentuated in correspondence with the accompaniment; i.e. trills unaccented, without *Nachschlag*
55	finish the phrase on f′; then take a breath to continue with the contrasting *molto cantabile*
57	bb, not b♮ in the *gruppetto* (note that this would otherwise clash with the Bb in the bass-line); the conventional rhythm usually employed for this ornament (quaver, triplet semiquaver, quaver, quaver) might be amended thus: crotchet, tied to first note of

a sextuplet of demisemiquavers (*cf* Fig 64); *diminuendo* throughout

60   3rd beat f, a quavers *molto staccato* to match VI

62-63   *sempre staccato*; arguments against the conventional slurring in pairs are that staccato leaps are a regular and unique characteristic of bassoon writing; additionally *staccato* offers better audibility

64   breathe after c′; the three appoggiaturas heavily accented, timed as 'triplet-syncopes'

65   trill without *Nachschlag*

66-68   take into consideration the disposition of the accompanying string chords by avoiding accents on 2nd or 3rd beats in bar 66, on 2nd or 4th beats in 67

68   this frequently occurring figure of a series of falling seconds would have been traditionally slurred in pairs; in this instance we should slur the 2nd, 3rd and 4th groups

69   suggested ornamenting: arpeggio flourish connecting c to g′ (Fig 61):

Fig 61

70   trill on g′ (not g!), starting on g′ rather than on a′, with *Nachschlag* at close

80,84   the note at the octave on the 2nd beat is unaccented, as in bars 35, 45

88   the appoggiatura accented, timed as a 'triplet-*syncope*'; trill without *Nachschlag*

93	the 5th repetition leads in a different direction to that of the preceding four figures; it thus deserves greater emphasis
97	the e' and f' forms the *Nachschlag* of a trill (otherwise un-notated) on f'; the *Einspielung* (lead-in) here might well lead directly into the tutti, with an *accel.* into tempo to indicate to the accompanying orchestra when to resume (Fig 62):

Fig 62

112-17	as in bars 45-50
120-24	as in bars 51-54
126,28,30	staccato quavers in response to the oboes
132,33	the altered VI passage obviates the need to make an echo of the repetition
136	trill without *Nachschlag*
138,139	quavers very short, mirroring VI in bars 59, 60
141,42	as in bars 62, 63
143	the appoggiaturas well accented, timed as 'triplet-*syncopes*'
144	start trill on upper note, trill without *Nachschlag*
145	note that VI,V2 take over from the top of the arpeggio on the 3rd beat
146,47	accentuation as in accompaniment; i.e. in bar 146 without accents on 2nd or 3rd beats

148,49	the lack of a punctuated accompaniment here, the *quasi fermata* effect of the sustained wind chord affords the soloist freedom to play with agogic; e.g. taking time over the repeated figure (which is treacherously awkward anyway!), and in the downward arpeggio accelerating back into tempo
150	as in bar 69: suggested ornamenting: an arpeggio flourish connecting F to c′ (Fig 63):

Fig 63

151	*crescendo*, trill here with *Nachschlag*
160	The pattern of omitting any *Einspielung* but inserting instead a lengthy cadenza, anachronistic in both style and technical demands, seems less relevant today than in former times. If *Einspielungen* are adopted, then the cadenza need not assume such a status.

II. Andante ma adagio

Note that modern mutes dampen the tone of the violins and violas more than period ones did in the 18th century.

The temptation to fill in every sequence of disjointed leaps with ornament (by analogy with such piano concertos as K491 i) should be resisted; however it might be tasteful to introduce a few (see bars 44-45)

7,8 the same appoggiatura ornament appears three times; its third appearance is traditionally concealed, but this for no convincing reason; e′, a should be unaccented in *diminuendo*

9 The first beat is f, not d (as in some modern editions); breathe after a; both the interspersed rests in the violins and the 4th beat silence in the bass indicates a lack of any accent in the solo-line

10 regarding the *gruppetto* ornament: the formula usually adopted (quaver, triplet semiquaver, quaver, quaver) can sound routine and inexpressive; try replacing with crotchet, tied to first note of a sextuplet of demisemiquavers (Fig 64):

Fig 64

note that to play b♮ lacks euphony and must be incorrect, as this clashes with the B♭ in the bass; the terminal f should be shortened in order to avoid clash with F♯ in the bass

11 as an 8′ register instrument, the bassoon may fittingly incorporate bass-function notes into the solo-line in a way that would be foreign to a 4′ instrument; thus such notes as the low F should not necessarily be phrased so as to form an integral part of the melodic line, but appear in parenthesis

12 trill to commence on upper note, without *Nachschlag*, with *diminuendo*

211

The Bassoon

13	This reiterated figure may be phrased according to its melodic contour – with an accent-*diminuendo* on the initial d, growing on the 2nd beat, an accent-*diminuendo* on the 3rd, and a *diminuendo* on the 4th beat (i.e. the *legato* group of three semiquavers does not form an up-beat to what follows). The semiquavers marked with staccato dots should be short and light, rather than lengthy and ponderous, so as to match the style of the violins (reiterated up-bows) and oboes.
14	expression by means of nuance, a graduated vibrato also being called for here
16	the slur covering the e g g′ on the 3rd beat is arguably incorrect, e forming the culmination of a descending sequence of sixths, while the phrase commencing g g′ g′ is taken up in imitation by the violins in the following bar; therefore snatch a breath after e
17	1st beat staccato semiquavers to be played short and light, mirroring the light bow-strokes of the upper strings in the following bar
17-18	the four pairs of semiquavers accompany the upper strings, and should not be interrupted by a breath; the lead is resumed at the 3rd beat of 18, and is best signified by taking a breath just before, i.e. after the b♮, which can hopefully sustain the phrase through to 20
20	a *Nachschlag* to be added to this trill; *senza crescendo,* since the *NMA* shows the 3rd beat still in *piano* (unlike the parallel situation in bar 47)

23	for the next two bars a darker mood prevails, characterized by both the modulation to a minor key and the use of syncopes; f♯ without accent
24	crotchet b♮ without accent
25	as the pair of syncopated notes C g′ seem to stand on their own, breathe only after the g′
26	g short and unaccented, matching the orchestral winds
28	stealing in, in imitation of VI
31	taking over once again from VI
33	terminate with a quaver, to avoid clash with bass
34	as in the case of bar 11, F does not form part of the phrase; accent, *diminuendo* on 3rd beat, so as to correspond with the bass part
35	D *forte*, d′ *piano,* to match accompanying strings; 3rd beat as in bar 34
36	B♭′ *forte*, b♭ *piano* as in bar 35; 3rd beat as in bar 34
34-36	this three-bar sequence modulating downwards from F major, d minor to B♭ major demands a progressive growth in intensity
37	trill commencing on upper note, slurred to g, with *diminuendo*
38-39	as in bars 13-14
42	the phrase must not be broken for breath after the 1st beat, but rather after the 3rd beat; corresponding to bars 16-17, the phrase terminates on a, being imitated in the following bar by the upper strings.
43	corresponding to bar 17
44	corresponding to bar 18
44-45	corresponding to bars 18-19; suggested embellishment (Fig 65):

Fig 65

45	corresponding to bar 19, breathe after d' to indicate new phrase commencing on the 6/4 chord
46	the phrase should be broken for breath neither after d' nor f'
47	for the record, the original 1805 edition (and all subsequent editions published into the 20th century by André) gives the following (Fig 66). Rudorff's amended version of 1881, which he justifies with "*muß offenbar so heissen*", has been adopted without question ever since. A *Nachschlag* is to be added to this trill; with *crescendo*, unlike the parallel passage in bar 20

Fig 66

49	in the circumstances it is merely a brief cadenza without modulation that is called for here; with regard to its end, note that the succeeding *tutti* bursts in *forte* (e.g. Fig 67):

Fig 67

III. Tempo di Menuetto

1	note that a *Tempo di Menuetto* indicates a measured pace that is other than fast
33-36	a developing of *crescendo*, of vibrato, is called for here
37-39	note that as these three bars clearly form a *ritmo di tre battute*, the breath must not be taken after the d′ in 38, but rather after the e in bar 39
42	the repetition, without accompaniment, of the preceding bar calls for some exercise of musical wit
45-48	the first triplet-quaver of each bar belongs to the preceding phrase
60,62	the *fp* in the accompanying strings must be reflected in the solo-part
71-72	*rall ... a tempo*
97,99	note the trills restored in *NMA* to both a♭ and b♭
103	any echo-effect attempted here is clearly out of place, given the imitation in VI
106	e′, f′ form the *Nachschlag* to the trill that is called for on f′; an *Eingang* leading into bar 107 needs to be inserted (e.g. Fig 68):

Fig 68

107-18	this passage, the only time that the theme is entrusted to the bassoon, calls for imaginative characterisation
119	staccato: *cf* 1st movement bars 62-63
121,123	as in bar 119
126-29	corresponding to bars 33-36

130-132   corresponding to bars 37-39: the breath must be taken after the trill in bar 132, rather than after e♭′ in bar 131

135   corresponding to bar 42, with an even heightened effect this time

136   some embellishment seems called for here: an arpeggio 8-note arabesque descending to F, rising to d′ is suggested (Fig 69):

Fig 69

137   with turn; with *crescendo* to correspond to that of the strings

138-50   play *col bassi*.

§5.2.2 Performance Notes on the Weber Bassoon Concerto op.75

In this tuneful work Weber has given us a vehicle reflecting the widest range of mood and expression of which the instrument is capable. The rapid changes of mood often call for kaleidoscopic changes of colour. The following guidelines on performance are intended to alert the player to these, rather than to offer specific suggestions regarding phrasing and articulation.

The 25 year old Weber wrote this concerto in Munich between 14th and 27th Nov. 1811. A fair copy of this version survives. 11 years later Weber had it engraved in parts, taking the opportunity of making a few minor revisions. Some 40 years after his death the same publisher issued a re-edited version, this time with piano accom-

216

paniment, on which all subsequent editions have been based. At first sight Weber appears inconsistent with his markings. It is evident however that, while meticulously marking certain passages, elsewhere he has deliberately left his interpreter free to determine matters of articulation and accentuation according to his own preference and technique. It has since become the rule for editors to decide all such matters on behalf of the player, failing to allow him to distinguish between what the composer has prescribed and what has been added. In the process of modernizing the notation, subtle indications of phrasing can also become lost. In 1990 an *Urtext* edition of the solo part with piano reduction appeared edited by the present author (Universal Edition UE 18131) restoring Weber's original markings. This edition supersedes earlier editions and should now be used in preference to any other. See also the article *Weber's Bassoon Concerto op. 75* (Waterhouse, 1986).

I. Allegro ma non troppo

1-40	the mood of the opening *tutti*, with its strongly defined dotted rhythms, sets an almost military mood to which the wistful 2nd subject forms the clearest contrast. The unaccompanied drum taps in bars 38-39 set a mood of theatrical expectancy
41-48	the military spirit is best served by sustained minims, crisp dotted rhythms and short crotchets. The lightly scored accompaniment requires no forcing of the tone.
42	the rhythm of the 3rd beat should probably correspond to that of bar 2
47,48	*diminuendo*, to offer the maximum contrast to the *fortissimo* tutti interjection
47	crotchets a, b both staccato – trill without *Nachschlag*
52-53	the use of the minor mode, in contrast to

	the major of 43-44, calls for some lyricism here
55-57	each of the three phrases progressively louder, in response to the *crescendo* in the strings
59	this is the first instance where the composer has refrained from specifying the articulation
61	trill without *Nachschlag*
62	trill with *Nachschlag*
67	the mood, firstly military and then virtuose, now changes to one of introspection
68	on the 3rd beat, note that Weber has indicated phrasing by giving the two quavers separate flags, rather that a single beam
70-71	the two bars of introspection are answered by a virtuose response marked *brillante* before resuming as before
74	the upbeat introduces a sustained expressive phrase which is matched in the accompanying strings
78- 82	scope for viruosity is offered here
88	as in 41, the stage is set for the contrasting second subject, in which wistful sentiment is combined with playfulness
95	the shortened third beat and accented fourth beat of the upper strings designate the time that should be taken over the pair of dotted rhythms
103-118	opportunities for considerable *bravura* are offered here
108	note the care with which the accents, beamings and slurs have been indicated
111	Weber wittily pitches a melodic D a tenth below the effective bass
113-118	The juxtaposing of both extremes of regis-

ter and of the extreme low register in quick succession would have provoked a considerable effect at the time, which the composer seeks to heighten by leaving unaccompanied. The culminating *fortissimo* C evokes a matching response from the orchestra before the movement continues. Adequate time must be taken for all of this to make its maximum effect.

147	a marking of *con fuoco* introduces a contrasting mood here
166-170	the presentation of the instruments lowest note – doubtless a superior note on the instrument at this time – has been artfully stage-managed in order to enable the soloist to demonstrate its maximum sonority
171	the response, marked *dolce*, and heightened by the grouping of flag and beam in 173, calls for powers of eloquence
180	note the craftiness with which the recapitulation is introduced, almost by stealth
186	Weber calls for a *Nachschlag* here
232	The effect achieved in bar 113 is duplicated and heightened by allowing the soloist to sound here his very highest note. Both then as now this passage requires adequate time taken to achieve its maximum effect.

II. Adagio

The theatrical atmosphere is maintained by an almost operatic cantilena, which should be compared with certain slow soprano arias from his operas. The tasteful use of agogic and vibrato can help to achieve the noble seriousness and idealised sentiment that calls for expression here.

17	the dramatic resumption of the opening prepares for the contrasting middle section

219

21   though the accompaniment remains as in bar 5, the solo line, in contrasting minor, is *più agitato* and starts with the theatrical gesture of a two octave downward slur

29-40   the answer in the major is set with a highly original accompaniment of just two horns, calling for considerable eloquence and freedom of tempo

47-48   the fanfare-like response to the preceeding string chords needs sensitive care to be transformed into the opening melody note of the recapitulation

54   although no *gruppetto* is notated here, such a sequence of notes is a classic instance of where one might be inserted

60   the fact that Weber has neglected to add markings to the initial scale hardly indicates *staccato*, which would introduce a jarring element

61   the same holds good here; note that the antepenultimate g', which is a resolving dissonance, must be slurred to the f' onto which it resolves.

III. Rondo Allegro

2   the familiar reading of the final quaver as d' was in fact introduced by the ca1865 reprint; all the early source gives it as c', both here and in the parallel bar 126.

45   the changed pattern of accompanying figuration heralds a change of mood, typified by combined dots and slurs

82   at this moment the *con fuoco* bravour that began in bar 71 must be transformed briefly into a sustained *dolce*

87-89   following two dainty *staccato* crochets the

	dolce mood is rudely interrupted by a violent arpeggio from bottom to top whose culminating note in bar 89 is reinforced by a dotted rhythm
99	Weber's *espressivo* and scrupulous markings lend significance to this imaginative section
117-123	devices such as augmentation, fragmentation, hesitation make this return to the main theme perhaps the most witty section of the entire work
161	the strongly syncopated accents in *scherzando* make this episode almost grotesque; from 169 they are answered by more conventional passage work
227	the quotation of the second part of the main theme (bar 9-12) in the remote key of D♭ reintroduces the main theme for the last time (bar 237), leading to a comparatively conventional display of passage work to bring the concerto to a rousing conclusion.

§5.3   Pedagogical Material

Tutor

The average tutor will contain such elements as basic playing instructions, fingering chart, graded etudes and duets for student and teacher. Early 19th century tutors also offer valuable information on such matters as reed-making and ornamentation. Pride of place belongs to the *Nouvelle méthode de basson* (1803) by the virtuoso and teacher Etienne Ozi (1754-1813), one of a series commissioned by the recently founded Paris Conservatoire, which has been re-issued many times; his instructions on reed-making remain the most important source of its kind. The

The Bassoon

encyclopedic '*Art of Bassoon-playing*' by Carl Almenräder (1786-1843) (Almenräder, 1843) deals with the reformed model on which the *Heckelfagott* was later to be based; this remained in print until the 1930s and deserves a re-print today. The prolific bassoonist-composer Eugène Jancourt (1815-1900) was also an influential teacher; his *Méthode théorique et pratique pour le bassoon* dates from 1847 and a revised version in English from 1911. Julius Weissenborn (1837-1888) (Pl 15) planned a comprehensive work that was to comprise tutor, etudes and original works with piano accompaniment – an ambitious scheme that sadly was never realised. His *Praktische Fagott-Schule / Practical Bassoon School* appeared on its own in 1887, with revised editions in 1929 and 1950; for over a century this has remained the tutor in most general use. In England the *Practical Tutor for the Bassoon* from 1885 by the band-master Otto Langey (1851-1922) (who also published tutors for other wind instruments) was the leading tutor for the then current French-system instrument; re-edited versions (which include useful selections of solo parts) have remained in print ever since. The best tutor today for the *basson* is Maurice Allard's *Methode de basson* (1975). The monumental *Das Fagott: Schulwerk in sechs Bänden /The Bassoon: a Tutor in six Volumes* (1977-84) by Werner Seltmann and Günter Angerhöfer contains 90 graduated lessons in Volumes 1-3, duets in vol. 4, pieces with piano in vol. 5, while vol. 6 is devoted to contra; this is a compre-hensive and well-structured work (containing much spe-cially commissioned music) that is highly recommended.

Etude

A worthwhile etude might be defined as a vehicle for treating specific problems of technique – identifiable and ideally referred to by title – so as to provide an efficient

Plate 15
Bassoon teacher Julius Weissenborn (1837-1888), active Leipzig 1857-87 in the Gewandhaus orchestra and 1882-88 at the Conservatorium

means of mastering them; the student is thus persuaded that time spent learning it will be purposefully directed and wisely invested. Bassoon etudes have been published in the past in considerable quantities – and are still being produced today. Sadly all too few satisfy these basic criteria:

- they fail to target any specific set of technical problems, being too diffuse in conception

The Bassoon

- they are written by teachers without aspirations to be composers – thus few are musically rewarding
- when containing figurations that undergo enharmonic permutations, coverage is hardly comprehensive.

The etude should supply a bridge between what is a mere technical routine and a piece of art music, being study material presented in artistic form. They can cover a wide range, from what is little better than a technical rigmarole to the 'concert study' or caprice, musically strong enough to stand concert performance. There are some well thought-out cycles of etudes that try systematically to cover a well-defined field of study; carefully conceived and graded, these guarantee progress when studied consistently in their prescribed order. The bassoonist is fortunate in possessing such a collection in the two volumes of *Bassoon Studies* first published by Julius Weissenborn in 1887. Although these remain the most used of all bassoon etudes it should be pointed out that, in the case of the second volume (*for Advanced Players*), his plan for a progressive order of difficulty was frustrated by the original publisher who issued them jumbled up and lacking their explanatory titles. The three sets of etudes (1894-95) by Louis Milde form an invaluable pendant to these, as do those of Eugène Jancourt (1847). It may be remarked that all three men were active as composers, Milde giving up bassoon-playing in later life to teach keyboard and composition.

In a class of their own are the sets of *Caprices* by the two outstanding composer-performer bassoonists of their time: the set by François Réné Gebauer (1773-1845) appeared in both Paris and Leipzig in 1809, while those by the German Carl Jacobi (1791-1852) were published in 1836. These are brilliant, idiomatic and, like those for violin by Paganini, satisfying as solo pieces. Another noteworthy etude is that written by Joseph Fröhlich (1780-1862) to exemplify the range of expression available in 1829 on the 9-keyed instrument. These have all been re-printed in *30 Classical Studies for Bassoon* (Waterhouse, 1987). The transcribing of etudes designed for one instrument onto another was a practice known in the past (*cf* Paganini-Liszt) and in the 1880s violin etudes by Kreutzer, Rode, Mazas and others were issued in bassoon arrangements in Paris. However it is exercises for voice rather than for violin – such as those by Concone – that are of greater relevance and value to the modern bassoonist (see §4.12 *Theory*).

Ensemble

The duet for student together with his teacher is a pattern hallowed by long tradition and one to be highly recommended (e.g. in Weissenborn, 1887). The bassoon ensemble – works for trio and larger group – forms a vehicle whereby students can learn multiple musical skills in an enjoyable fashion (e.g. Milde, Dubois).

Sight-reading

The final *concours* of the Paris conservatoire traditionally included, in addition to the *morceau imposé*, a piece of specially commissioned sight-reading with piano accompaniment; composers of the stature of Bizet and Massenet were not above accepting such commissions. A selection was published for the first time in *Paris Conservatoire Sight-Reading Pieces* (Waterhouse, 1992). Three of these derive from a remarkable set of 135 written 1913-15 by Eugène Bourdeau (1850-1928) for his twice-weekly Conservatoire class (as yet unpublished). This tradition had been established by his predecessor Jancourt, many of whose *morceaux à dechiffrer* composed 1876-91 with accompaniment for a second bassoon also survive.

The Bassoon

Orchestral Passages

The danger of relying on published albums rather than the orchestral parts themselves – given that these frequently contain *retouchements* and misprints – has already been pointed out (see §4.17 *Audition*).

Six
Bibliography & Work-lists

§6.1 Articles and Books

Allard, Maurice, *Methode de bassoon* (Paris, 1975)

Almenräder, Carl, 'Ueber die Erhaltung der Fagottrohre', *Caecilia* Bd xi (1829) 62

Almenräder, Carl, *Die Kunst des Fagottblasens oder Vollständige theoretisch praktische Fagottschule* (Mainz, 1843)

Bartholomäus, Helge, *Das Fagottensemble: kleines Handbuch zur Musikpraxis* (Berlin, 1992)

Bartolozzi, Bruno, *New Sounds for Woodwind* (Oxford, 2\1982)

Beebe, Jon P., *Music for unaccompanied Solo Bassoon: an annotated Bibliography* (Jefferson NC, 1990)

Belfrage, Bengt, 'Blechbläser-Sportler', *Brass Bulletin 21* (1978)

Benade, Arthur, *Fundamentals of Musical Acoustics* (Mineola NY, 2\1990)

Brand, Erick D., *Band Instrument Repairing Manual* (Elkhart IN, 8\1978)

Brindley, Giles, 'The Logical Bassoon', *Galpin Society Journal* XXI (1968) 152-61

Brown, Edgar, 'Another Look at the Bassoon', *Double Reed News* 42 (1998) 8-10

Bubnovich, Venceslav Mikhailovich, *Aktualnuie problemui ispolnitelstva na fagote* (Barnaul, 1996)

Bulling, Burchard, *Fagott Bibliographie* (Wilhelmshaven, 1989)

Burton, James Lee, *Bassoon Bore Dimensions* (diss. U. of Rochester NY, 1975)

Camden, Archie, *Bassoon Technique* (London, 1961)

Campbell, J. Patricia, 'Musical Instruments in the Instrumentälischer Bettlermantl – a Seventeenth-Century Musical Compendium', *Galpin Society Journal* XLVIII (1995) 156-67

Carroll, Paul, *Baroque Woodwind Instruments* (Aldershot, 1999)

Christlieb, Don, *Notes on the Bassoon Reed: Machinery, Measurement, Analysis* (Los Angeles CA, 2\1966)

Cooper, Lewis Hugh & Toplansky, Howard, *Essentials of Bassoon Teaching* (Union NJ, 1968)

Cooper, L. Hugh, 'How is your Bassoon?', *International Double Reed Society Journal* ii (1974) 7-20

Cuciureanu, Gheorghe, 'The Future of the Cuciureanu System Bassoon', *The Double Reed* 8.2 (1985) 24-33

Eubanks, Mark G., *Advanced Reed Design & Testing Procedure for Bassoon* (Portland OR, 3\1993)

Fox, Alan, 'Defining the Two Types of Bassoons – Long and Short Bore', *The Instrumentalist* (Nov. 1968) 53-54

Fröhlich, Joseph, *Systematischer Unterricht* (Würzburg, 1829)

Gieseking, Walter & Leimer, Kurt, *Piano Technique* (London, 1972)

Hähnchen Dieter, *Zeitgenössische Musik für Fagott solo* (Leipzig, 1985)

Haynes, Bruce, *The eloquent Oboe: a History of the Hautboy from 1640 to 1760* (Oxford, 2001)

Heinrich, Jean-Marie: *Contribution à l'étude de l'anche du basson,* (diss. Université Paris, 1987)

Heinrich, Jean-Marie, *Recherches sur les propriétés densitométriques du matériau Canne de Provence et ses similaires étrangers* (unpublished 1991)

Heyde, Herbert, 'Contrabassoons in the 17th and early 18th century', *Galpin Society Journal* XL (1987) 24-36

Hindemith, Paul, *Elementary Training for Musicians* (London, 1946)

Jansen, Will, *The Bassoon: its History, Construction, Makers, Players and Music* (Buren, 1978)

Jooste, Stephanus J., *The Technique of Bassoon Playing: an evaluative and methodological Study* (Potchefstroom, 1984)

Joppig, Gunther, *The Oboe and the Bassoon* (London, 1988)

Kenyon de Pascual, Beryl, 'The Dulcians (Bajón and Bajoncillo) in Spain: an updated Review', in Lasocki, D. (ed.), *A Time of Questioning: Proceedings of the International Double-Reed Symposium Utrecht 1994*, (Utrecht, 1999)

Kergomard, Jean, 'Acoustique du basson', *Bulletin du groupe d'acoustique musicale Nos. 82 & 83* (Paris, 1975-76)

Kilbey, Maggie, *Curtal, Dulcian, Bajón: a History of the Precursor of the Bassoon* (St Albans, 2002)

Koch, Heinrich Christoph, *Musikalisches Lexikon* (Frankfurt-Main, 1803)

Koenigsbeck, Bodo, *Bassoon Bibliography / Bibliographie du basson* (Monteux, 1994)

Kopp, James, 'Precursors of the Bassoon in France before Louis XIV', *Journal of the American Musical Instrument Society* XXVIII (2002) 63-117

Krüger, Walter, 'Akustische Grundlagen des Fagotts und der Oboe', *MGG2* s.v. 'Fagott'

La Borde, Pierre de, *Essai sur la musique* (Paris, 1780)

Langwill, Lyndesay G., *The Bassoon and Contrabassoon* (London, 1965)

Lipori, Daniel G., *A Researcher's Guide to the Bassoon* (Lampeter, 2002)

McKay, James R., *The Bassoon Reed Manual: Lou Skinner's Theories and Techniques* (Bloomington IN, 2000)

Moennig, W. Hans, 'Bassoon Maintenance', *To the World's Bassoonists* 2.3 (1972) 3

Moyse, Marcel, *Tone Development through Interpretation for the Flute* (Tokyo, 1971)

Neklyudov, Yuri, 'O konstruktivnuikh usovershenstvovaniyakh fagota', *Metodika obucheniya igre na dukhovykh instrumentakh #11* (Moscow, 1966)

Nekliudov, Yuri, 'Practical Points for Improvement of the Bassoon', *International Double Reed Society Journal* i (1973) 18-27

Neukirchner, Wenzel, *Theoretisch practische Anleitung zum Fagottspiel* (Leipzig, 1840)

Norris, Richard, *The Musician's Survival Manual: a Guide to Preventing and Treating Injuries in Instrumentalists* (Saint Louis MO, 1993)

Ouzounoff, Alexandre, *Actuellement le basson: traité pratique des nouvelles techniques au basson* (Paris, 1986)

Ozi, Etienne, *Nouvelle méthode de basson* (Paris, 1803\R1974)

Pace, Temistocle, *Ancie battente* (Florence, 1943)

Penazzi, Sergio, *Metodo per fagotto* (Milan, 1972)

Penazzi, Sergio, *Il fagotto: altre techniche* (Milan, 1982)

Phillip, Robert, *Early Recordings and musical Style* (Cambridge, 1992)

The Bassoon

Popkin, Mark & Glickman, Loren, *Bassoon Reed Making* (Northfield IL, 2\1987)

Riedelbauch, Heinz, *Systematik moderner Fagott- und Basson-technik: Bassonographie, Veränderung von Einzeltönen und Mehrklangtechnik* (Celle, 1988)

Righini, Fernando, *Il repertorio del fagotto* (Florence, 1988)

Scherchen, Hermann, *Lehrbuch des Dirigierens* (Leipzig, 1927)

Schilling, Gustav, *Aesthetik der Tonkunst* (Mainz, 1838)

Schulze, Werner, 'Kontra Streich: Versuch einer Neubewertung der Neben-Instrumente des Fagottisten', *fagott forever: Karl Oehlberger zum achtzigsten Geburtstag* (Wilhering, 1992)

Seltmann, Werner, & Angerhöfer, Günter, *Das Fagott* (Leipzig, 1977–84)

Sherwood, Thomas, *Starting on an Early Bassoon* (Cambridge, 1998)

Smith, David Hogan, *Reed Design for early Woodwinds* (Bloomington IN, 1992)

Taffanel, Paul & Gaubert, Philippe, *Methode complète de flûte* (Paris, 1923)

Terëkhin, Roman, *Shkola igry na fagota* (Moscow, 1981)

Waterhouse, William, 'Weber's Bassoon Concerto op. 75: the manuscript and printed Sources compared', *International Double-Reed Journal* (1986) 46-56

Waterhouse, William, 'A critical Bibliography of historical teaching Material for Bassoon 1700-1900: Tutor, Chart and Etude', *fagott forever: Karl Oehlberger zum achtzigsten Geburtstag* (Wilhering, 1992)

Waterhouse, William, *The New Langwill Index: a Dictionary of Musical Wind-Instrument Makers and Inventors* (London, 1993)

Waterhouse, William, 'Bassoon', *The New Grove Dictionary of Music and Musicians* (London, 2\2001)

Weber, Rainer, 'Early Double Reeds', *Galpin Society Journal* LIV (2001) 233-41

Weber, Rainer, 'Early Double Reeds: Postscript', *Galpin Society Journal* LVI (2003) 280-81

Weait, Christopher, *Bassoon Reed-making: a basic Technique* (New York, 2\1980)

Weisberg, Arthur, 'A double automatic octave Key System for the Bassoon', *The Double Reed* 24.3 (2001) 93-94

Weissenborn, Julius (ed. Waterhouse), *Fagott-Studien op 8.2* (Vienna, 1985).

White, Paul, 'Early Bassoon Fingering Charts', *Galpin Society Journal* XLIII (1990) 68-111

White, Paul, 'Early Reed Design', in Lasocki, D. (ed.), *A Time of Questioning: Proceedings of the International Double-Reed Symposium Utrecht 1994*, (Utrecht, 1999) 189-203

White, Paul, 'The Bass Hautboy in the Seventeenth Century', in Lasocki, D. (ed.), *A Time of Questioning: Proceedings of the International Double-Reed Symposium Utrecht 1994*, (Utrecht, 1999) 167-82

Wolf, Guntram, 'The new Contrabassoon in 2002 – a new Design', *Double Reed News* 60 (Autumn 2002) 26-28

§6.2 Recommended Repertoire

This select list, together with that of §6.3, offers a comprehensive overview of such items of the repertoire that should merit performance today. With few exceptions only original works for dulcian / bassoon have been included. It is of necessity a personal choice, with a preponderance of 'early' over 'late' period material; it will hopefully be found to exclude little of comparable value found among the vast quantity of works listed by Bulling and Koenigsbeck in their reference books. For convenience it is divided into sections.

Bassoon & Basso continuo: author of realisation given in brackets; duets *a due* (with obligato right hand) are excluded.

Bassoon & Keyboard: Sonatas, Suites: any work in several movements is included here.

Bassoon & Orchestra: solos primarily conceived with orchestral accompaniment are listed, rather than under those with piano. It should be noted that many are available in piano reduction only, rather than in full score.

The Bassoon

Date: that of composition, rather than of publication, is given; in many cases this can be little more than an informed guess (e.g. ca 1800).

Publisher: chosen, where applicable, on the basis of reliability (see below). Where no modern edition – or one that is a reliable reprint – currently known, the place / date of original printing is given in brackets.

The bassoonist's problem with regard to worthwhile music to play is that

- there is less of it than for most other instruments
- much of it is either out of print or otherwise unavailable
- it is often only available in a flawed edition.

The ways in which such editions may be flawed include:

- littered with misprints
- misunderstanding by the editor of the original text
- in 18th century music unstylish realization and omission of figures
- gratuitous / anachronistic editings, such as the adding of dynamic and other markings
- source / editorial procedures not divulged.

In marked contrast to the situation with other wind instruments, virtually no item of key literature is available in facsimile reprint today. It was due to the initiative of the author that the first such publication appeared (Galliard 6 Sonatas, Bassoon Heritage Edition, 1989).

However there has been a gratifying growth in recent times in the number of publications of historic literature, together with a marked improvement in editorial standards. Nonetheless many of the best works will be currently out of print and thus only accessible via a specialist library. The restricted market for bassoon publications has traditionally made them unattractive to large commercial publishers. Especially affected is repertoire from the ear-

232

liest period; some valuable works have remained unpublished since the 17th century and are only available in microfilm or in facsimile. However access these days to the necessary source-material via reference book, library and internet has fortunately never been easier. Through the growth of 'period' ensembles and the influence of radio, there has been a spreading of knowledge through stylish recordings; re-prints of period treatises and urtexts have made available much of the necessary source-material. The result is that there is less excuse these days for performances to rely on poor editions, while those that do may justifiably be criticized.

It is to be hoped that the existence of so much worthwhile repertoire that is potentially performable in public will deter the soloist from having to rely on the use of transcriptions and encourage initiative in programme-building. With regard to the large number of lesser-calibre works – such as what may be termed 'study' concertos – included here, these will enable the teacher to adopt a syllabus that proceeds through the repertoire in an orderly way, whereby the few masterpieces we possess can be approached in their proper context.

Bassoon (unaccompanied)

ACKER Dieter	Monodie [1967]	Breitkopf & Härtel
ALLARD Maurice	Variations sur un thème de Paganini [1986]	Billaudot
APOSTEL Hans Erich	Sonatine op 19.3 [1953]	UE
ARNOLD Malcolm	Fantasy [1966]	Faber
BARTOLOZZI Bruno	Collage [1970]	Suvini Zerboni
BENTZON Jørgen	Studie i variationform op 34 [1940]	Hansen
BERIO Luciano	Sequenza XII [1997]	UE
Anon. (attrib. Braun)	24 Capricen [1740]	Amadeus
BRAUN Jean (attrib.)	Pièces sans Basse [1740] (facsimile)	S.P.E.S.
BRUNS, Victor	4 virtuose Stücke op 93 [1991]	Feja
DINESCU Violeta	Satya II [1984]	Astoria
GEBAUER François Réné	6 Caprices [ca1809] (*30 Classical Studies*)	UE

233

The Bassoon

(ed. HÄHNCHEN Dieter)	Album *Musik des 20. Jahrhunderts*	Breitkopf & Hartel
HOLLIGER Heinz	Three Pieces [2002]	Schott
JACOB Gordon	Partita [1969]	OUP
JACOBI Carl	6 Caprices op 15 [1836] (*30 Classical Studies*)	UE
KOLBINGER, Karl	Vortrag [1994]	k.o.m. Muskverlag
MACONCHY, Elizabethy	Excursion (1985)	Chester
MIGNONE Francisco	16 Valsas [1981]	Funarte
OSBORNE Willson	Rhapsody [1958]	Peters
OZI Etienne	42 Caprices [1803]	Hofmeister
PERSICHETTI, Vincent	Parable IV op 110 [1970]	Elkan-Vogel
SESTAK Zdenek	5 virtuosic inventions [1966]	Panton
STOCKHAUSEN Karlheinz	In Freundschaft [1983]	Stockhausen
TCHEREPNIN Nicolai	Esquisse op 45.7a [1921]	Omega
TON-THAT Tièn	Jeu des Cinq Eléments II [1982]	Jobert
YUN Isang	Monodie [1983/84]	Bote & Bock

Bassoon & Basso continuo

BERTOLI Giovanni A.	9 Sonatas [1645] (facsimile)	Musedita
BESOZZI Jerome (attrib.)	Sonata in B♭ [ca1765] (Waterhouse)	OUP
BÖDDECKER Philipp F.	Sonata sopra la Monica [1651] (Waterhouse)	UE
CORRETTE Michel	6 Sonates (les Délices de la Solitude) op 20 [ca1739]	(Paris ca1739)
DARD Marcel	6 Sonatas op 2 [1767]	(Paris 1767)
DEVIENNE Francois	6 Sonatas op 24 [ca1785]	(Paris ca1785)
FASCH Johann F.	Sonata in C [ca1740/50] (Haselböck)	UE
GALLIARD John E.	6 Sonatas [1733] (facsimile)	Bassoon Heritage
HEINICHEN Johann D.	Sonate in D [ca1725] (Bernstein)	Peters
MERCI Louis	6 Sonatas [ca1735]	(London 1735)
PFEIFFER Franz A.	6 Sonatas [ca1785] (Rhodes)	Piper Publications
PLEYEL Ignace	6 Solos [ca1795]	(Paris ca1795)
SALAVERDE Selma y	Canzona per fagotto solo [1638] (facsimile)	S.P.E.S.
TELEMANN Georg P.	Sonata in f [1728] (Michel)	Amadeus
–	2 Sonatinen [1731] (Müller)	Schott

Bassoon & Keyboard: Sonatas, Suites

AMON Johann	Sonata [ca1810]	Amadeus
BACH P.D.Q.	Sonata abassoonata [1996]	Presser
BRANDL Johann E.	Sonate op 42.1 [ca1825]	UE
BRUNS, Victor	Sonate op 20 [1949]	Pro Musica
–	Sonate #3 op 86 [1988]	Feja

CASTELNUOVO-TEDESCO Mario	Sonatina [1946]	GMP
CHALLAN Henri	Sonatine [1937]	Selmer
COOKE Arnold	Sonata [1987]	Emerson
DÜRNITZ Thaddeus von	6 Sonatas [ca1775]	Accolade
DUNHILL Thomas	Lyric Suite op 96 [1941]	Boosey & Hawkes
HURLSTONE William Y.	Sonata [1904]	Emerson
KOECHLIN Charles	Sonate op 71 [1918/19]	Billaudot
KRUFFT Nikolaus von	Grande Sonate op 34 [1818]	Accolade
LISTE Anton	Grande Sonate op 3 [1807]	UE
LONGO Alessandro	Suite op 69 [1915]	Accolade
MOSCHELES Ignaz	Grande Duo Concertante op 34 [1816]	Musica Rara
MOZART Wolfgang A.	Sonata K292 (arr. Waterhouse) [1775]	Chester
REICHA Anton	Duo op post. [1810/15]	Schott
SAINT-SAENS Camille	Sonata op 168 [1921]	Durand
SCHAFFRATH Christian	Duetto in f [ca1750]	Heinrichshofen
–	Duetto in g [ca1750]	Schott
SCHICKELE Peter	Summer Serenade [1993]	Elkan-Vogel
SCHRECK Gustav	Sonata [ca1880]	Hofmeister
SKALKOTTAS Nikos	Sonata Concertante [1943]	Margun
TANSMAN Alexandre	Sonatine [1952]	Eschig
–	Suite [1960]	Eschig
THEUSS Karl T.	Sonatine [1820]	(Leipzig 1820)
WATERHOUSE Graham	Diplo-Diversions op 44 [1998]	Hofmeister

Bassoon & Keyboard: Pieces

ALMENRÄDER, Carl	Potpourri op 3	Bassoon Heritage
–	Intro & Vars. op 4	Bote & Bock
BAINES Francis	Introduction & Hornpipe [1950]	Schott
BAIRD Tadeusz	4 Preludia [1957]	PWM
BINET Jean	Variations sur un chant de Noël [1957]	Henn
BOURDEAU Eugène	1ère Solo [1894]	Leduc
–	2me Solo [1907]	Leduc
–	3me Solo [1920]	Leduc
BOUTRY Roger	Interférences I [1972]	Chappell
BOZZA Eugene	Récit, Sicilienne et Rondeau [1934]	Costallat
BRUNS, Victor	Concerto op 5 [1933]	Leeds Music Corp.
–	2. Konzert op 15 [1946]	Hofmeister
–	5 Stücke op 40 [1965]	Breitkopf & Härtel
BÜSSER Henri	Récit et Thème varié op 37 [1909]	Leduc
–	Pièce de Concours op 66 [1917]	Leduc
–	Cantilène et Rondeau op 75 [1925]	Leduc

The Bassoon

DEMERSSEMAN Jules	Introduction & Polonaise op 30 [ca1860]	Accolade
DUTILLEUX Henri	Sarabande et Cortège [1942]	Leduc
DWARIONAS Balys	Thema und Variationen [1952]	Sikorski
ELGAR Edward	Romance op62 (arr. pf) [1909]	Novello
FRANÇAIX Jean	Deux Pièces [1996]	Schott
FUČIK, Julius	Concertino op131 [1893]	ms
GALLON Noël	Récit et Allegro [1938]	Oiseau-Lyre
GLIERE Reinhold	Impromptu, Humoresque op35.8, 9 [1908]	IMC
GODFREY Fred	'Lucy Long' Variations [ca1880]	Boosey & Hawkes
GROVLEZ Gabriel	Sicilienne et Allegro giocoso [1930]	Leduc
IBERT Jacques	Carignane [1953]	Billaudot
–	Morceau à dechiffrer [1921]	ms
JACOB Gordon	4 Sketches [1977]	Emerson
JACOBI Carl	Introduction & Polonaise op 9 [1829] (arr. pf)	Musica Rara
JANCOURT Eugene	Etude melodique op 79 [ca1870]	Emerson
KALLIWODA Johann W.	Morceau de Salon op 230 [ca1860]	Accolade
KATZER Georg	Moment musical [1966]	Gravis
KOECHLIN Charles	3 Pieces op 34 [1898/89]	Billaudot
KOSTLAN Ivan	Concert Etudes 1–2 [1961], 3-4 [1962]	Moscow
LALLIET Théophile	Fantaisie brillante op21 [ca1890]	Costallat
MASSENET Jules	Morceau à dechiffrer [1882] (*Sight-Reading Pieces*)	UE
MERCADANTE Saverio	Cavatina [1848]	aka Verlag
MILDE Louis	3 Easy Pieces [ca1890] (*Bassoon Solos vol.1*)	Chester
–	3 Study Pieces [ca1890]	Musica Rara
–	Tarentella op 20 [ca1890]	Musica Rara
–	Polonaise [ca1890]	Musica Rara
–	Concertino in a [ca1890]	UE
NUSSIO Otmar	Variazioni su un'arietta di Pergolesi [1953]	UE
PIERNÉ Gabriel	Solo de Concert op 35 [1898] (arr. pf)	Leduc
–	Prélude de Concert (sur Purcell) [1933]	Salabert
RENÉ Charles	Solo de Concert [1901] (arr. pf)	Lemoine
ROSSINI Gioacchino (attrib.)	Allegro [ca1845]	UE
RUMMEL Christian (L.A.)	Variations [ca1817]	(Mainz ca1817)
SEMLER-COLLERY Jules	Récitatif et Final [1951]	Eschig
SPOHR Louis	Adagio op 115 [1817]	Schott

236

Bibliography & Work-lists

STAROKADOMSKY Mikhail	4 Pieces op25 [ca1950]	IMC
TCHEREPNIN Nicolai	Esquisse op 45.7 [1921]	Omega
VINTER Gilbert	Reveriê [1952]	Cramer
–	The Playful Pachyderm [1942]	Boosey & Hawkes
WATERHOUSE William (ed.)	*Paris Conservatoire Sight-Reading Pieces*	UE
–	*Bassoon Solos vol.1*	Chester
WATERSON James	Souvenir de Donizetti [ca1865]	Nova
WEISSENBORN Julius	Romanze op 3 [1882]	Forberg
–	6 Vortragsstücke op 9 [1888]	Hofmeister
–	3 Vortragsstücke op 10 [1888]	Breitkopf & Härtel
–	Capriccio op 14 [1888]	IMC
–	5 kleine Stücke [1888]	Hofmeister

Bassoon & Voice

BACH Johann Christian	'Non m'alletta' (*Temistocle*) (tenor, bn, orch) [1772]	
BACH Johann S.	'Lass mich kein Lust' (Cantata 177) (tenor, bn, bc) [1732]	
BOYCE William	'Softly rise' (*Solomon*) (baritone, bn, orch) [1742]	(London 1742)
CHABRIER Emanuel	'l'Invitation au voyage' op.post. (sop, bn, pf) [ca1890]	Costallat
CHERUBINI Luigi	'Ah, nos peines' (*Medée*) (sop, bn, orch) [1797]	(Paris 1797)

Bassoon & Orchestra (* = strings only)

ADDISON John	Concertino [1998]	Emerson
BACH Johann Christian	Concerto in B♭ [ca1772]	Editio Musica
–	Concerto in E♭ [ca1772]	Editio Musica
BARTOLOZZI Bruno	Concertazioni [1964]	Suvini Zerboni
BERWALD Franz	Concertstuck op 2 [1827]	Bärenreiter
BITSCH Marcel	Concertino [1948]	Leduc
BOND Capel	*Concerto in B♭ [1746]	Boosey & Hawkes
BOZZA Eugene	Concertino op 49 [1946]	Leduc
BRANDL Johann E.	Concertino in F [ca1820]	Karl Hofmann
BRUNS, Victor	3. Konzert op 41 [1966]	Breitkopf & Härtel
CRUSELL Bernard	Concertino [1829]	Fazer
DANZI Franz	Concerto in F [ca1815]	Leuckart
–	– in g [ca1815]	Accolade
–	– in F [ca1815]	Sikorski
DAVID Ferdinand	Concertino op12 [1839/40]	Hofmeister
DEVIENNE François	Concerto [ca 1795]	Hofmeister
ELGAR Edward	Romance op 62 [1909]	Novello
FASCH Johann F.	Concerto in C [ca1750]	Heinrichshofen

The Bassoon

FIALA Joseph	Concerto in C [ca1800]	Kunzelmann
FOGG Eric	Concerto [1931]	Emerson
FRANÇAIX Jean	*Concerto [1979]	Schott
FUČIK, Julius	*Polka: Der alte Brummbär op 210 [1907]	Apollo
GRAUN Johann Gottlieb	*Concerto in B♭ [ca1750]	Sikorski
GRAUPNER Christoph	*Concerto in G [1743]	Hofmeister
–	*- in c [ca1744]	Barenreiter
GRØNDAHL Launy	Concerto [1942]	Dania
GUBAYDULLINA Sofia	*Concerto [1975]	Sikorski
HARGRAVE Henry	*5 Concertos [1762]	Phylloscopus
HAYDN Michael	Concertino [ca1770]	Doblinger
HERTEL Johann Wilhelm	Concerto 1 in B♭ [ca1780]	Phylloscopus
–	– 2 in E♭ [1789]	Phylloscopus
HUMMEL Johann N.	Concerto in F [ca1810]	Boosey & Hawkes
JACOB Gordon	*Concerto [1949]	Stainer & Bell
JACOBI Carl	Concertino op 7 [1828]	Musica Rara
–	Introduction & Polonaise op 9 [1829]	Musica Rara
JOLIVET André	Concerto [1954]	Heugel
KALLIWODA Johann W.	Variations & Rondeau op 57 [1856]	Eulenburg
KELEMEN Milko	*Concerto [1958]	UE
KOZELUCH Anton	Concerto in C [ca1775]	Musica Rara
KREUTZER Conradin	Variations KWV4202 [ca1815]	UE
LARSSON Lars-Erik	*Concertino op 45.4 [1957]	Gehrman
LINDPAINTNER Peter von	Concerto in F [ca1850]	Accolade
MACONCHY Elizabeth	*Concertino [1968]	Lengnick
MILDE Louis	Concerto ♯2 in f [ca1890]	Musica Rara
MOLTER Johann Melchior	*2 Concertos [ca1750]	Accolade
MOZART Wolfgang A.	Concerto in B flat K191/186e [1774]	Bärenreiter
– (attrib.)	Concerto ♯2 KA230/196d [ca1800]	Peters
MÜTHEL Johann Gottfried	Concerto [ca1770]	Bote & Bock
OZI Etienne	Concerto ♯5 op11 [	Salabert
PAUER Jiri	Concerto [1958]	Artia
PFEIFFER Franz Anton	Concerto in B♭ [ca1785]	Leuckart
PHILLIPS Burrill	*Concert Piece [1940]	C.Fischer
PIERNÉ Gabriel	Solo de Concert op 35 [1898]	Kalmus
PLEYEL Ignace	Concerto in B♭ [ca1775]	Musica Rara
RÖSSLER (ROSETTI) Franz Anton	Concerto in B♭ [ca1785]	Simrock
–	– in B♭ [ca1785]	Schott & Co
RENÉ Charles	Solo de Concert [1901]	Lemoine
ROSSINI Gioacchino (attrib.)	Concerto [ca1845]	Hofmeister

238

Bibliography & Work-lists

SPISAK Michael	*Concertino [1957]	Ricordi
STAMITZ Carl	Concerto in F [ca1780]	Piper Publications
TOMASI Henri	Concerto [1957]	Leduc
VANHAL Johann B.	Concerto in C [ca1790]	Simrock
VERDI Giuseppe	Capriccio [ca1833]	ms
VILLA-LOBOS Heitor	*Ciranda das sete notas [1933]	Southern
VINTER Gilbert	Concerto [1969]	ms
VIOLA Anselmo	*Concerto in F [ca1790]	Heinrichshofen
VIVALDI Antonio	*39 Concertos [ca1720]	Ricordi
WEBER Karl M. von	Concerto in F op 75 [1811/22]	UE
–	Hungarian Rondo op 35 [1813]	UE
WINTER Peter	Concerto in c [ca1813]	Joseph Acs
WOLF-FERRARI Ermanno	Suite-Concertino op 16 [1933]	Ricordi

Two Bassoons & Orchestra

DIETTER Christian Ludwig	Concerto in B♭ [ca1785]	Doblinger
JOHNSEN Hinrich P.	*Concerto [1751]	Editions Viento
MÜTHEL Johann G.	Concerto in E♭ [ca1770]	Schottstädt
RITTER August	Sinfonia Concertante [1806]	Braach
SCHACHT Theodor von	*Sinfonia Concertante [ca1815]	Phylloscopus
TOLLER Ernst O.	Concerto [ca1850]	Accolade
VANHAL Johann B.	Concerto in F [ca1790	Musica Rara

Concertante

FRANÇAIX Jean	Quadruple Concerto (fl, ob, cl, bn) [1935]	Schott
HAYDN Joseph	Symphonie Concertante (ob, bn, vn, vc) [1792]	Breitkopf & Härtel
HINDEMITH Paul	*Concerto (tpt, bn) [1949]	Schott
MOZART Wolfgang A. (attrib.)	Symphonie Concertante K297b (ob,cl,hn,bn) [1778]	Breitkopf & Härtel
PAGANINI Nicolo	Pezzo da Concerto (hn, bn) [1813]	Musica Rara
STRAUSS Richard	*Duet-Concertino [cl, bn] [1947]	Boosey & Hawkes
TELEMANN Georg P.	*Concerto in F (recorder, bn) [ca 1740]	Breitkopf & Härtel

Bassoon Duo

ALMENRÄDER Carl	2 Duos op 9 (2bn) [1810]	Jack Spratt
–	2 Duos op 10 (2bn) [1810]	Accolade
BIZET Georges	Morceau à dechiffrer (bn, vc) [1874]	Musica Rara
BOISMORTIER Joseph B. de	6 Sonates op 14 (2bn) [1726]	Amadeus
–	6 Sonates op 40 (2bn) [1726]	(Paris 1726)
–	Petites Sonates op 50 (2bn) [1734]	(Paris 1734)
COUPERIN Francois	13. concert (2bn) [1724]	Oiseau Lyre
GEBAUER Francois R.	6 Duos concertant op 25 (2bn) [ca1805]	Bassoon Heritage

The Bassoon

GOEPFERT Karl Andreas	Sonate (bn, guitar) [1806/07]	Bote & Bock
GUBAYDULLINA Sofia	Duo Sonate (2bn) [1977]	Sikorski
HINDEMITH Paul	Stücke (bn,vc) [1942]	Schott
–	Duo (bn, cb) [1927]	Schott
JACOBI Carl	2 Duets op 5 (2bn) [1826]	Musica Rara
JANCOURT Eugène	6 Sonates progressives (2bn) [1847]	Costallat
MOZART Wolfgang A.	Sonata K292/196c (bn, vc) [1775]	Breitkopf & Härtel
OZI Etienne	6 petites sonates, 6 grandes sonates (2bn) [1803]	Accolade
PAGANINI Nicolo	3 Duetti concertanti (vn, bn) [ca1800]	Suvini Zerboni
PFEIFFER Franz Anton	2 Duettos (vn, bn) [ca1785]	Piper Publications
RITTER Georg W.	Duetto in F (2bn) [ca1800]	Piper Publications
ROUSSEL Albert	Duo (bn, cb) [1925]	Durand
SCHOBERT Johann	6 Sonatas or Duets (2bn) [ca1745]	Bassoon Heritage
SELTMANN & ANGERHOEFER.	*Das Fagott Bd iv: Duette* (2bn)	Breitkopf & Härtel
STRAVINSKY Igor	Lied ohne Name (2bn) [1918]	Boosey & Hawkes

Bassoon Trio

BANTOCK Granville	Dance of Witches [1927]	Swan & Co.
–	The Witches' Frolic [1927]	Goodwin & Tabb
BERGT Adolf	Trio [ca1860]	Hofmeister
BOZZA Eugene	Divertissements [1954]	Leduc
BRUNS Viktor	Trio op 97 (tenor bn, bn, cbn) [1992]	Feja
FUCHS Georg Friedrich	6 Trios Concertants [ca1810]	Lemoine
GEBAUER François R.	Trios Nos.1–6 [ca1830]	Accolade
–	Trio No.7 [ca1830]	Feja
HAAN Stefan de	Trio [1959]	Feja
MILDE Louis	14 Trios [ca1890]	UE
SPEER Daniel	2 Sonaten [1687]	Nova
WEISSENBORN Julius	6 Stücke op 4 [1882]	Musica Rara

Bassoon Quartet

ADDISON John	4 Miniatures [ca1970]	Emerson
BACH P.D.Q.	Last Tango in Bayreuth [1973]	Presser
–	Lip my Reeds [1993]	Presser
BRUNS Viktor	Kleine Suite op 55 (3bn, cbn) [1974]	Breitkopf & Härtel
–	– op 68 (3bn, cbn) [1981]	Breitkopf & Härtel
–	3. Kleine Suite op 92 (3bn, cbn) [1990]	Feja
CORRETTE Michel	Le Phénix Concerto [4bn, BC] [ca1738]	Carus

DUBOIS Pierre Max	Scherzo [1963]	Leduc
–	Histoires de basson [1977]	Billaudot
GEVIKSMAN Vitaly	Prelude & Fugue [1960]	Moscow
HABA Alois	Quartet op 74 [1951]	CHF Praha
HUMMEL Johann N.	Quartet [ca1810]	Feja
JACOB Gordon	Prelude, Fugue & Scherzo [1979]	Emerson
KOLBINGER Karl	Variationen nach J.Haydn [1981]	Hieber
LAUBER Joseph	Divcrtimento [1945]	Feja
PROKOFIEV Sergei	Scherzo Humoristique op 12.9 [1912]	Forberg
RIDOUT Alan	Pigs [1973]	Emerson
SCHUMAN William	Quartettino [1939]	Peer
WAGENSEIL Georg C.	6 Sonaten (3bn, cbn) [ca1760]	Doblinger
WATERHOUSE Graham	Hexenreigen op 45 [1996]	Accolade

Solo Chamber Music

AHO Kalevi	Quintet (bn, str 4tet) [1977]	Fazer
BAX Arnold	Threnody & Scherzo (bn, str 4tet, cb, hp) [1934]	Chappell
BRANDL Johann E.	Quintet op 14 (bn, vn, 2 va, vc) [1798]	Strube Verlag
–	2 Quintets op 52 (bn, vn, 2 va, vc) [1826]	Accolade
–	3 Quintets op13, 61, 62 (bn, pf, vn, va, vc) [ca1796]	Strube Verlag
BRUNS Victor	Konzertante Musik op 58 (bn, str 4tet) [1982]	Breitkopf & Härtel
DANZI Franz	3 Quartets op 40.1, 2, 3 (bn, str trio) [ca1814]	Musica Rara
DEVIENNE François	3 Quartets op 73 (bn, str trio) [1797]	Amadeus
FIALA Joseph	2 Trios (bn, vn, vc) [ca1800]	Feja
FRANÇAIX Jean	Divertissement (bn, str 4tet, cb) (1942)	Schott
GEBAUER François R.	Trio op 33.3 (bn, vn, vc) [ca1810]	Musica Rara
JACOB Gordon	Suite (bn, str. 4tet) [1969]	Musica Rara
JACOBI Carl	Quartet op 4 (bn, str trio) [1826]	Accolade
KROMMER Franz	2 Quartets op 46.1, 2 (bn, 2va,vc) [1804]	Amadeus
REICHA Anton	Grand Quintet (bn, str 4tet) [1826]	Phylloscopus
–	Variations (bn, str 4tet) [ca1826]	Phylloscopus
RITTER Georg W	6 Quartets (bn, str trio) [ca1777]	(Paris ca1777)
SCHWARTZ Elliott	Chamber Concerto V (bn, pf, str 4tet) [1992]	ms
STAMITZ Carl	2 Quartets op19.5,.6 (bn, str trio) [ca1777]	Musica Rara

The Bassoon

| VOGEL Johann C. | Quartet op 5.1 (bn, str trio) [ca1785] | Musica Rara |
| WESTRUP Jack | Divertimento (bn, vc, pf) [1948] | Augener |

Contrabassoon (unaccompanied)

BAUR Jürg	Arabesken, Girlanden, Figuren [1990]	Breitkopf & Härtel
SCHULHOF Erwin	Bassnachtigall [1922]	Emerson, Schott
WATERHOUSE Graham	Contraventings op 46 [1998]	Hofmeister

Contrabassoon & Piano

BRUNS Viktor	2 Stücke op 57 [1975]	Breitkopf & Härtel
–	6 Stücke op 80 [1986]	Breitkopf & Härtel
–	Conzertante Suite op 95 [1991]	Feja
WATERHOUSE Graham	Aztec Ceremonies op 37 [1996]	Hofmeister

Contrabassoon & Orchestra

BRUNS Viktor	Concerto [1992]	ms
NUSSIO Otmar	*Divertimento [1978]	ms
SCHULLER Gunther	Concerto [1977]	AMP

§6.3   Recommended Pedagogical Material

Tutor

ALLARD Maurice	*Méthode de basson / The Bassoon*	Billaudot, Paris 1975
ALMENRÄDER Carl	*Die Kunst des Fagottblasens oder Vollständige theoretisch praktische Fagottschule*	Schott, Mainz 1843
JANCOURT Eugène	*Méthode théorique et pratique pour le bassoon*	Richault, Paris 1847
– (ed. Fitz-Gerald J. & James, E. F.)	*Bassoon School*	Hawkes, London 1911
LANGEY Otto	*Practical Tutor for the Bassoon*	Hawkes & Son, London 1885
OZI Etienne	*Nouvelle méthode de basson*	Paris 1803 /R
SELTMANN Werner & ANGERHöFER Gunter	*Das Fagott: Schulwerk in sechs Bänden /The Bassoon: a Tutor in six Volumes*	Breitkopf & Härtel, Leipzig 1977 - 1984
WEISSENBORN Julius	*Praktische Fagott-Schule/ Practical Bassoon School*	Forberg, Leipzig 1887

242

Bibliography & Work-lists

– (revised Schaefer, C.)	*Praktische Fagott-Schule / Practical Bassoon School*	Forberg, Leipzig 1929
– (revised Bettoney F.)	*Method for Bassoon*	Bettoney, Boston MA 1950

Etude

CONCONE, Giuseppe (ed. Emerson J.)	*The Singing Bassoon: 40 legato studies*	Emerson, Ampleforth 1999
FRÖHLICH, Joseph	*Allegro maestoso* (Würzburg 1829) in *30 Classical Studies*	UE, Vienna 1987
JANCOURT, Eugène (ed. Waterhouse, W.)	*26 Melodic Studies*	UE, Vienna 1987
MILDE, Louis	*Studien über Tonleiter und Akkord-Zerlegungen op 24*	Hofmeister, Leipzig ca1895
–	*50 Koncert-Studien Op 26 Heft 1, Heft 2*	Hofmeister, Leipzig ca1895
WATERHOUSE, William (ed.)	*30 Classical Studies for Bassoon*	UE, Vienna 1987
WEISSENBORN, Julius	*Fagott-Studien / Bassoon Studies Op 8/1 for Beginners*	Peters, Leipzig 1887
– (ed. Waterhouse, W.)	*Bassoon Studies Op 8/2 for Advanced Pupils*	UE, Vienna 1985

Ensemble

WATERHOUSE, W. (ed.)	*Bassoon Duets*	Chester Music, London 1983

Sight-reading

WATERHOUSE, W. (ed.)	*Paris Conservatoire Sight-Reading Pieces*	UE, Vienna 1992

Orchestral Passages

KOLBINGER, Karl, & RINDERSPACHER, Alfred (ed.)	*Test Pieces for orchestral Auditions*	Peters, Frankfurt 1992
MORELLI, Frank (ed.)	*Stravinsky: difficult Passages for Bassoon*	Boosey & Hawkes, New York 1997
PIESK, Gunter (ed.)	*Orchesterstudien: Mahler*	Zimmermann, Frankfurt 1988
RIGHINI, Fernando (ed.)	*Il fagotto in orchestra*	Firenze 1971
SCHOENBACH, Sol (ed.)	*20th Century Orchestra Studies*	Schirmer, New York 1970
STADIO, Ciro (ed.)	*Passi difficili e "a solo"*	Ricordi, Milano 1932
TURKOVIC, Milan (ed.)	*Orchesterstudien: Schönberg, Berg, Webern*	UE, Vienna 1997

Seven
Appendices

§7.1 Appendix I: Chronicle

It may be argued that our musical instincts and standards
are essentially derived from experience – environments we
have worked in and those who have influenced us. What
follows sets out my credentials as performer and teacher
and lists those to whom artistically I feel most indebted.

Training

My main teachers were Archie Camden for bassoon and
Gordon Jacob for theory. The former, influenced whilst a
student by the pianist Egon Petri, imbued a pre-occupation
with finger technique which was later to prove valuable. A
'natural' himself, he offered limited guidance to students
with problems of breath-leading; in this respect I was res-
cued by a horn player, the later conductor Alan Abbott.
Severe problems of playing position were ultimately
resolved by adopting a crook with modified bend and
spike, inspired by a course of lessons in the Alexander
Technique. I later benefitted from coaching by Steven
Maxym (New York), Sol Schoenbach (Philadelphia), Hugh
Cooper (Ann Arbor), Enzo Muccetti (Milan), Mordechai
Rechtman (Tel Aviv), and from attending classes given by
Karl Oehlberger (Vienna), Maurice Allard (Paris) and
Marcel Moyse (Canterbury). I studied reed-making with
Kurt Ludwig (Munich) and Louis Skinner (Baltimore).

Teaching

As Tutor in bassoon at the Royal Manchester (later Royal Northern) College of Music I taught bassoon from 1966 to 1996; also as guest professor in 1972 at Indiana University, Bloomington for nine months, and in 1984 at the Victoria College of the Arts, Melbourne, Australia for three months. I have given Master-classes at Tanglewood, Banff, Haus Marteau (D-Lichtenberg) etc.

Competitions

I competed in Munich 1958, Geneva 1959 and Prague 1960 – and served as Juryman at *ARD* Munich in 1965, 1975, 1984 and 1990, Prague 1986, Markneukirchen 1990 etc.

Bassoonist

Philharmonia Orchestra under Guido Cantelli, Wilhelm Furtwängler, Herbert von Karajan and Arturo Toscanini.
Royal Opera House Covent Garden under Ernest Ansermet, Rudolf Kempe, Clemens Krauss.
RSI (CH-Lugano) under Sergiu Celibidache, Hermann Scherchen and Carl Schuricht.
London Symphony under Antal Dorati, Jascha Horenstein, Josef Krips, Pierre Monteux, George Solti and Leopold Stokowski.
BBC Symphony under Pierre Boulez and Gennadi Rozhdestventsky.
As free-lance under Sir Thomas Beecham and Victor de Sabata.
Melos Ensemble of London – numerous concert tours and recordings.
Concerto performances with Sir Adrian Boult.

The Bassoon

Artists worked with have included:

Composers: Benjamin Britten, Aaron Copland, Jean Françaix, Paul Hindemith, Gordon Jacob, Zoltan Kodaly, Bruno Maderna, Luigi Nono, Karlheinz Stockhausen, Igor Stravinsky, Michael Tippett, Ralph Vaughan Williams and William Walton

Singers: Maria Callas, Dietrich Fischer-Dieskau, Kirsten Flagstad, Tito Gobbi, Peter Pears, Joan Sutherland and Renata Tebaldi

Pianists: Wilhelm Backhaus, Emil Gilels, Glenn Gould, Arturo Michelangeli, Sviatoslav Richter, Arthur Rubinstein and Rudolf Serkin

String players: Yehudi Menuhin, Nathan Milstein, David Oistrakh, Leonard Rose, Mstislav Rostropovich, Isaac Stern, Henryk Szering and Josef Szigeti

Wind players: Marcel Moyse, Leon Goossens, Gervase de Peyer and Dennis Brain.

§7.2   Appendix II: The Author's Instrument

The following modifications, incorporated over years of playing, serve to illustrate just one example of changes that are possible. Most professional bassoonists modify their instruments to suit their own style and needs.

Specification

Made 1938 by Heckel, Biebrich – model 41i @ A = 440Hz, No.8224 (Pl 16); fitted with neither rollers nor high d″ key, but with e/f♯ trill key and LH5 crook-key on the wing-joint. Pad centres treated with paraffin wax, pad seatings varnished.

Plate 16
The Author demonstrating his playing position, bend of crook and spike
Photograph: Edward Webb

The Bassoon

Crook

- Specification: non-standard model, built ca1953 to order
- Length: 310mm (i.e. somewhat shorter than standard)
- Tip: somewhat wider (0,43mm diameter); wall chamfered to knife-edge thickness at rim; lapped with fine thread to ensure air-tight seal
- Nipple: original pin-hole enlarged to 1mm diameter by Hans Moennig
- Shape: relatively straight, with obtuse angle governed by considerations of required angle of reed entry and hand comfort.*

Wing-Joint

- Crook-key flap: elongated to accommodate the crook in permanent pulled-out position
- LH1 keys: the four touches bent so as to lie closely adjacent to each other; the height of the 'a'-key touch lowered to facilitate hopping over it by the thumb
- LH3 key: touch bent so as to allow it to be simultaneously opened while stopping the hole
- LH4 'brille': aperture width allows mechanism to operate with finger stopping hole (if required)
- Inner edge: wood filed away to allow long-joint to be rotated, bringing the low D touch closer to that of the c♯ for the LH1
- LH1: crook-lock
- LH5: additional crook-key.**

* benefits conferred include freedom from condensation problems in either crook or finger-holes
** this supplementary crook-key, besides freeing the LH thumb for other duties and largely replacing the crook-lock, allows the crook pin-hole to be closed whenever the LH1 harmonic keys are in use. Interestingly this device was first proposed by Jancourt in the mid 19th century and has been adopted by the French bassoon ever since.

248

Butt-Joint

- RH3: pad of 'brille' mechanism in cork
- RH4: B♭ key touch bent, angled laterally to facilitate G-B♭ slurring
- RH5 touches: extended to accommodate finger access
- RH1 touches: heights adjusted to accommodate finger access
- Hand-rest: purpose designed, mounted to accommodate hand access
- Butt-cap: fitting to accept adjustable spike silver-soldered on at side
- U-bend bow: brass mount caulked with flexible sealant; rubber gasket replaced with cork
- Bore: ascending bore adjacent to U-bend bow varnished
- RH1 E-key: thumb support ledge removed.

Case

Modified so that for ventilation purposes the RH5 A♭ key on the butt remains wedged open.

§7.3   Appendix III: The Bending of Crooks

If making a major change to the shape of crook is contemplated then this is best left to the professional repairman. Parts where the curvature is more pronounced – i.e. where the tube is at the largest diameter – are the greatest at risk; the repair patches often seen on the side of old crooks betray where the seam at the side has sprung apart due to an intolerable strain having been placed on it.

If only a minor adjustment needs to be made it should be possible to undertake this oneself. The first step is to establish in advance the precise shape required. This may be done by first making an imitation crook with which to experiment using a piece of electric cable of suitable length and stiffness – or a draughtman's 'flexicurve' – (an inexpensive item obtainable from most drawing-office suppliers). Draw on paper the existing shape of crook by using it as a template; super-impose the new shape. This will indicate where the alteration has to be made.

If the degree of alteration is slight and confined to the narrower part of the tube then this can be undertaken as follows. Grasp the crook with both hands, thumbs applied laterally at the centre of the bend and index fingers above. With extreme care 'encourage' the bend by pulling with the index fingers while at the same time pushing with the thumbs. Under no circumstances should pressure be merely applied from the thumbs – otherwise a kink may well result.

If the degree of alteration is more extreme then it will be necessary to fill it first with a low melting alloy. This is the process adopted in manufacture after the tube has been formed on the straight mandrel. The tube will now bend as if it were a solid bar. The alloy can then be melted out under a hot water tap and retained for future re-use. These types of fusible metal (alloys containing bismuth and lead) start melting at a temperature as low as 46° Celsius (117° Fahrenheit) and solidify at room temperature, expanding very slightly in the process of cooling. A small iron pot and a hot-plate is all that is needed. The material can be bought by the pound in small ¼ pound ingots which have their melting point cast into the surface.

Index of Plates

Index of Plates

Index of Names

Index of Names

Index of Names

Index of Names